Eat Well for 99¢ A Meal

by Bill & Ruth Kaysing

Loompanics Unlimited
Port Townsend, Washington

This book is sold for information purposes only. Neither the author nor the publisher will be held accountable for the use or misuse of the information contained in this book.

Eat Well for 99¢ A Meal
© 1996 by Loompanics Unlimited

All rights reserved. No part of this book may be reproduced or stored in any form whatsoever without the prior written consent of the publisher. Reviews may quote brief passages without the written consent of the publisher as long as proper credit is given.

Published by:
Loompanics Unlimited
PO Box 1197
Port Townsend, WA 98368
Loompanics Unlimited is a division of Loompanics Enterprises, Inc.

Cover design by Shaun Hayes-Holgate

ISBN 1-55950-137-5
Library of Congress Card Catalog 95-95-81315

Contents

Introduction by Steve Schumacher i

Foreword To The Second Edition iv

Dedication v

Preface To The Second Edition vi

Author's Note vii

Foreword 1

Part 1
    How To Shop On 99¢ Per Meal 7

Chapter One
    What To Buy To Stock Your Pantry 9

Chapter Two
    Where To Shop And How To Do It 25

Chapter Three
    How To Develop Your Bargaining Skills 35

Chapter Four
    Where To Pick Fresh Foods For Free 39

Chapter Five
    Your Kitchen Is Your Workshop 49

Chapter Six
    Food You Can Grow Yourself 59

Chapter Seven
    How To Preserve Your Perishables 73

Chapter Eight
    In Case You Have To Use A Supermarket 81

Chapter Nine
    What You Should Know About Sugar 89

Part 2
How To Cook For 99¢ A Meal 95

Chapter Ten
The Golden Rule: Eat Less, Waste Nothing 97

Chapter Eleven
Sample 99¢ Menus 103

Chapter Twelve
Enjoy Better Bread By Making Your Own 123

Chapter Thirteen
The Noble Spud To Your Budget's Rescue 129

Chapter Fourteen
Soybeans: The Money-Saving Meat Substitute 135

Chapter Fifteen
Recipes From Around The World 143

Chapter Sixteen
Healthful Desserts From Simple Ingredients 163

Chapter Seventeen
A Checklist Of Health And Money-Saving Hints 169

Recommended Reading 187

Index 193

Introduction
by Steve Schumacher

I'm the son of the son of the son of Ferdinand Schumacher, founder of the Quaker Oats Company before he sold it to its current owners. So here's a food comparison that resonates for me.

Quaker Oats sells in my local supermarket for $1.99 an 18 ounce can, complete with a nice picture of an avuncular Quaker and a slogan saying "nothing is better for thee than me." And in truth, this simple can of rolled oats is one of the most wholesome and economical choices on the sugar-smackin' supermarket cereal shelf. (Which is, unfortunately, not saying much.)

But turn a few blocks away to my friendly neighborhood food co-op — for the last two months it's been selling organic rolled oats for 29 cents a pound. That's $0.29 compared to $1.99 a pound, less than one sixth the price and to my mind a far superior product. After all, these 29-cent oats are organically-grown, meaning they're free of chemical pesticides and fertilizers — a healthy food carefully harvested in healthy soil.

This comparison epitomizes for me the message of Bill & Ruth Kaysing's fine book, ***Eat Well For 99¢ a Meal***. Even at its best, conventional supermarket fare is a bad deal. You can eat far better and cheaper by getting your food from alternative sources.

Simply put, you can upgrade your food supply if you forego pricey, packaged, processed foods and instead buy basic foods in bulk, or else grow or wildcraft them yourself. The Kaysings survey this whole field and show you how to dine in style, with tasty recipes galore — so "back to basics" doesn't mean chowing down on hard red wheat three meals a day! The emphasis is on how to eat well, not just cheaply.

Eat Well On A Dollar A Day was written in 1975 and brought up-to-date for this new edition. Despite all the inflation over the past 20 years, I was surprised that several bulk foods have actually gone down in price. For example, brown rice in fifty-pound sacks cost about 40 cents a pound in 1975 — now you can get it for 30 cents a pound. Beans went for 40 cents a pound, but now go as low as 30 cents a pound. Peas were 22 cents a pound and are now 20 cents a pound. Rye has plummeted from 55 cents a pound to 20 cents a pound. And so on.

Actually, almost all bulk foods are much cheaper than 20 years ago if you correct prices for inflation. Chalk this up to improved farming techniques — although the American farmer herself has hardly benefited, reaping only about 22 cents on each dollar of retail food sales.

The closer you get to the farmer, whether by gardening yourself, shopping at farmer's markets, or buying in bulk, the closer you get to the true, low price of healthy food. The more you shop in supermarkets, the more you pay for and encourage chemical fertilizers, pesticides, processing, packaging, transportation, advertising, overhead, and executive salaries.

What with the general price level doubling or tripling, it may be harder to approach the Kaysings' 99¢-a-day ideal, but there are always options. Two days after being asked to write this foreword, I attended a natural food industry trade show. What a delightful capitalist Mardi Gras experience! For 6 hours I nibbled on delicious samples of expertly-prepared healthy foods that wholesalers eagerly offered me and my fellow retailers.

That same evening, I went to a fun university music recital, which was followed by a free reception replete with salads, asparagus spears, baklava, and desserts of every description.

Now that was a classic example of how to eat *very* well on *nothing* a day!

Foreword

To The Second Edition

As you will note, the bulk of this revised book remains the same as when it was first published (circa 1975). We attribute this to the fact that the basic principles have not changed significantly. Prices have changed but not the winning way of buying natural foods in bulk and preparing them yourself.

Dedication

Our deepest appreciation to our children and to the many others who contributed fresh and vital ideas.

Special mention to those who had the courage to taste our many experiments.

Bill & Ruth Kaysing

Preface

To The Second Edition

An invitation from Mike Hoy, President of Loompanics Unlimited, to us suggesting an update of *Eat Well On A Dollar A Day* generated a fast and enthusiastic response. That's because there is a great need for relevant information on the all-important subject of food. For example, millions of people are still smearing something worse than axle grease on their toast; it's called margarine and is loaded with hydrogenated oil which is now recognized as lethal to your cardiovascular system. More on this in the Checklist (Chapter Seventeen).

Yes, dear readers, the crisis in nutrition is more severe than when this book was first published in 1975. Not only are consumers being hijacked pricewise, they are cheated of food value in practically every category. Take packaged cereals — they often contain 50 percent sugar, a worthless non-food. In some instances, the fancy cardboard box in which they arrive has more nutrition than the heavily-processed cereal it contains!

Want more energy, more robust, vigorous health? Then you must eat food that can impart these well-being characteristics and this book will be your faithful guide. As an important bonus, you'll learn how to save lots of money. And though it is hard to believe, you'll learn how you can still enjoy three homemade meals for a cost of less than one dollar!

Take care of your health and it will take care of you.

Bill & Ruth Kaysing

Author's Note

Until I was forty (I am now seventy-two), I lived on a diet of plastic foods. It was a rare day in South Pasadena when, as a growing boy, I didn't consume at least four or five of my favorite candy bars. Fueled by these hunger-stoppers plus plenty of canned corn, hot tamales, and ice cream, I dragged through adolescence like a tired snail. I usually felt dull, sluggish, and hungry.

Not long after the Japanese attacked Pearl Harbor, I began to eat the United States Navy's fare. Big deal. Still no feelings of good health and exuberance. And I went from bad to worse. In 1950 I worked as an insurance adjuster in lovely Los Angeles, and I started my day three hundred and sixty-five times a year with a cream puff. Looking back, I'm sure that the physical and mental collapse I finally experienced was due to my abominable diet. But I *still* didn't wise up until about thirty years ago when my family began talking to me about wheat germ and yogurt and co-author Ruth showed me the way to good health and high spirits with a natural foods diet. Since that turn-around in my eating habits, I have never been as productive as I am now.

So take heart when you read these pages. If it can happen to me, it can certainly happen to you.

Foreword

Authors often give their works-in-progress nicknames. This one had two: "Eat" and "The Radical Gourmet." I like the latter because it implies that people are going to have to take what amounts to a radical political stance in order to fight against the blandishments of Madison Avenue and the lure of the supermarkets. We are increasingly required to fight the good fight in order to maintain our basic right to eat well for a reasonable amount of money. This means that we must constantly search for alternatives to the down-the-drain methods of buying and preparing food that the media and the food industries encourage.

If you are browsing in a book store and are just riffling through this book out of curiosity, consider this anecdote before you put the book down.

Susan Savvy goes on a marketing expedition and buys the following items for $10.00:

	Price per Pound	Amount Purchased	Total
Honey	1.19	1 pound	1.19
Potatoes	.29	8 pounds	2.32
Cheese	2.19	1 pound	2.19
Whole grain wheat	.29	10 pounds	2.90
Beans	.35	4 pounds	1.40
		24 pounds	$10.00

Eat Well For 99¢ A Meal

Here's what Pat Programmed buys at the local Plastic Food Mart for the same price:

Sugar-Frosted Flakes	1.6 pounds	$ 4.59
TV Dinner	0.6 pound	2.52
Large bag Chips	0.9 pound	2.89
	3.1 pounds	$10.00

Susan obtained twenty four pounds of healthful, basic, bulk foods for her ten dollars. Naturally, prices vary throughout the country and according to the season. These were obtained as the book went to press in Port Townsend, Washington. They are the listed prices at a local natural food store.

To assist the reader in comparing the actual food values in the purchases made by Sue and Pat, here are reproductions from a remarkably valuable pamphlet titled *Nutritive Value of Foods*. It is Home and Garden Bulletin Number 72 issued by the United States Department of Agriculture. To obtain a copy write to the U.S.D.A., Washington, DC 20250, for availability and price of a copy for your own use.

Readers can draw their own conclusions as to which shopper got the most food value for their ten bucks.

Need I say more? If so, be apprised of what we're up against.

Nutrients:	**What they do:**	**Where they are found:**
Protein	Builds and repairs all tissues. Helps form anti-bodies to fight infection.	Fish, poultry, milk, cheese, egg, dried beans and peas, nuts, peanut butter, soy, cereals, bread
Fat	Supplies a large amount of energy in small amount of food. Supplies essential fatty acids.	Butter, salad oils, dressings, cooking oil

Foreword

Carbohydrates	Supplies energy. Helps the body use other nutrients.	Cereals, breads, corn, grits, oats, macaroni, rice spaghetti, noodles, molasses, honey, syrup, jams
Minerals		
Calcium	Helps build bones and teeth. Helps clot blood. Helps muscles and nerves react normally.	Milk, yogurt, cheese, mustard and turnip greens, collards, kale, canned salmon and mackerel
Phosphorus	Helps build bones and teeth. Helps control the rate at which energy is released.	Milk, poultry, eggs, cereals, soy
Iron	Combines with protein to make hemoglobin, the red substance in the blood that carries oxygen to the cells.	Eggs, dried beans and peas, whole grain cereals and breads, dark green leafy vegetables, molasses
Water	Also essential, even though many people do not think of it as a food. Water helps in carrying the nutrients to cells and waste products away, in building tissues, regulating body temperature, aiding digestion and replacing daily water loss. Be sure it's pure.	
Vitamins	Essential for body growth, for resisting infection and for keeping the body functioning properly. All vitamins needed for good health can be found in food.	
Vitamin A	Helps keep skin clear and smooth. Helps eyes adjust to dim light. Helps keep lining of mouth, nose, throat and digestive tract healthy and resistant to infection.	Egg yolk, dark green leafy and yellow vegetables, deep yellow fruits, whole milk, yogurt, butter

Eat Well For 99¢ A Meal

Thiamin or Vitamin B1	Promotes good appetite. and digestion. Helps keep nerves in healthy condition. Helps change substances in food into energy for work.	Whole grain cereals, and breads, milk and cheese, soy
Riboflavin or Vitamin B2	Helps cells use oxygen. Helps keep vision clear. Helps keep skin around mouth and nose smooth.	Whole grain cereals and breads, milk, cheese, soy
Niacin	Helps keep nervous system healthy. Helps body cells use oxygen to produce energy. Helps to maintain the health of the skin, tongue and digestive system.	Whole grain cereals and breads, lean poultry, fish, peas and beans
Ascorbic Acid Vitamin C	Helps maintain intercell structure. Strengthens walls of blood vessels. Helps in healing wounds. Helps resist infection.	Oranges, grapefruits, limes, lemons, strawberries, cantaloupes, collard, mustard greens, cabbage, kale, green peppers, potatoes
Vitamin D	Helps the body absorb calcium. Helps build strong bones.	Vitamin D fortified milk, cod and halibut liver oil, salt water fish, mackerel, fresh or canned salmon

The American food industry is a $476.8 billion a year business. Somewhere between the farmer, who gets $105.3 billion, and the consumer who pays the $476.8 billion, there is a large leak of $371.5 billion. In other words, the middlemen who promote and sell the food and control the prices we pay for it make a gross profit of $371.5 billion a year. It is the purpose of this book to encourage you to help reduce this leak or plug it up altogether by providing two kinds of information: how to eat what your body

Foreword

needs and wants (not what the industry says it should need or want); and how to avoid paying into the pockets of the middleman.

To eat well you must learn how to outwit some very clever minds. The food-industry moguls and their hired guns, the dirty rats on Madison Avenue, are very good at what they do. They have managed to convince a huge proportion of the American people that we are getting our money's worth when we buy processed foods. They have accomplished this monumental feat (monumental considering the evidence to the contrary) in most cases by suppressing or simply ignoring the truth. To help you deal with these rascals, culprits, and con men, the bulk of this book will elaborate on these basic rules:

> When I submitted this paragraph, the original publisher, Phelps Dewey of Chronicle Books, said that if he printed it, the building would be bombed. He tried to persuade me to delete it or at least leave out phrases like "dirty rats, culprits and con men." I refused, stating that the book had to spell out the true facts or it would be worthless... in short, no pussyfooting and no punches pulled now or later. I was able to convince Phelps that we had an important message to transmit, one that involved life or death decisions. So the paragraph remained as written *exactly as it appears here and now.*

1. Plan on changing your entire way of life regarding food. No half-way measure will do if you really want to eat for less than a dollar a meal.
2. Develop a sense of humor as well as a sense of strategy. Think of yourself as a guerrilla in a funny/serious war with rats who are trying to profit from your presumed gullibility. But keep in mind that the last laugh will be yours, since you are fully capable of using your head in finding out the truth on your own.
3. Stay out of supermarkets except when shopping for fresh foods and possibly dairy products.
4. Search out and buy from alternative food sources (I cite some good ones in this book).

5. Plan on keeping lots of bulk foods in your home at all times. That way you will reduce your shopping trips and will be protected in case of disaster.
6. Be open-minded. Try new foods, both wild and domestic.
7. Plant a garden; the bigger it is the better for your pocketbook. There are good books on the subject in your local library and book store, and more are coming out all the time.
8. Learn about harvest times for local crops.
9. Think of meat as a condiment, not as a staple.
10. Give up sugar and all sugar-containing products. It's easier to do than you may think, and the reasons for doing it are pressing, as you will learn.
11. Buy international cookbooks. Find out what people in other cultures eat and try their recipes.
12. Eat raw foods or let things cook themselves. Save time and energy (yours and the kind you pay for).
13. Eat less. Determine your own minimum requirements and keep to them.
14. Don't waste anything.
15. Make your own convenience foods. You can even make money doing this if you're creative and enterprising enough.

As a side note, I want to emphasize that this book takes a positive approach to shopping and food preparation. It was designed to encourage you to change your ways by providing creative suggestions. Rather than labor the specific evils of packaged and processed foods, I refer you to Adelle Davis' *Let's Eat Right to Keep Fit* (New American Library) and D. Sanford's *Hot War on the Consumer* (Pitman).

Now read on for specific information. You'll feel better just knowing that you can win at the game the food industry plays with you for their profit.

Part 1

How To Shop On 99¢ Per Meal

Why Bulk Foods Are A Bargain

During the Great Depression, wheat sold for as little as 32¢ a bushel (55 lbs.) which was often far less than the cost of growing it. Today, wheat is selling for about $4 a bushel. However, when you correct the prices and quote it in terms of Great Depression prices, you find that wheat is really selling for about 40¢ a bushel! Advanced technology has fostered this unique turn of events. Thus, your real buys in today's food markets are the bulk grains, beans and other basic commodities. Thus, when you build your menus around these items, you'll enjoy eating well for *far less* than you ever thought possible!

Chapter One

What To Buy

To Stock Your Pantry

What You'll Learn:
What to buy for maximum economy and nutrition. Typical staples and basic foods.

Pioneering Americans learned how to ensure an adequate food supply for their families against all sorts of disasters and unpredictable events. They maintained a pantry with stocks of basic items such as grains, beans, nuts, and seeds. Then, no matter what happened — floods, Indian wars, poor harvests — they could survive and keep their strength up.

Anyone can set up a pantry at any time and almost anywhere. Create a space, building some shelves if you have to, find or buy some sealable containers, and with the basic staples listed on the following pages plus a supply of fresh foods to combine them with, you're all set. The Chinese and Mexican styles of cooking revolve around a well-stocked pantry with great success both economically and nutritionally. Take a look at some Chinese and Mexican cookbooks to get a sense of how you can work from the basics in your pantry to produce a great variety of inexpensive, healthful, and delicious meals. Your cooking will be simple and direct — almost nothing to it if you've stocked up thoroughly. And you will have automatically produced a healthy food environment for yourself and your family.

The rules to follow when setting up your pantry are simple:

- Buy basic foods that are easy to store without refrigeration.
- Buy in bulk.
- Avoid all packaged foods.
- Buy fresh vegetables and fruit to combine with your pantry staples.

The amount of purchase will vary from family to family, but we recommend buying as much as your storage space and budget permit. For example, a family of four could profit by purchasing five hundred pounds of wheat at one time, thereby undoubtedly getting a discount. It can be stored in clean cans, bottles or metal lined bins to prevent mice and rat attacks. With that purchase alone (remember, it increases fourfold when cooked) the family would have a reserve of more than a ton of excellent food on hand. If not eaten, it can be bartered for other foods, planted in the spring, parched (lightly roasted) as a snack or otherwise put to good use.

Here's a good general rule: Keep enough food stored to provide ten times the body weight of each family member (a 150-pound man needs 1500 pounds of food per year). This would ensure a one-year reserve of basic foods. But again, remember that dry foods make up three to five times their dry weight. Thus, less is needed as long as a plentiful supply of pure water is available.

Now to the specifics of what to buy to stock your pantry. You'll find recipes and suggestions on how to use these foods in subsequent chapters.

Chapter One
What To Buy To Stock Your Pantry

Build Your 99¢ A Meal Lifestyle With Wheat

Since wheat is one of the least expensive bulk foods and available everywhere, we suggest learning how to use it in many different ways. Recipes are provided courtesy of:

Meadowlark Grain Co.
PO Box 33
Hingham, MT 59528

who grow high-quality wheat on their Montana ranch. They supply it in sacks in any quantity you wish.

Whole Grain Wheat

Basic to most diets, wheat can be freshly ground for bread, rolls, pancakes, and other baked goods. It can be boiled whole (or slightly cracked) for cereal. Or it can simply be soaked to grow sprouts. However you choose to use it, a substantial quantity of whole grain wheat will provide a strong and solid foundation for your home food supply. Suggestions on how to use wheat will be found throughout this book.

Wheat Nuts or Popped Wheat

Raw wheat kernels (berries)	Cooking oil
Water	Seasoning

Clean and rinse wheat kernels. Place in a saucepan with enough water to cover. Bring water to a boil. Reduce heat to medium low. Steam kernels until they burst. This may take from 1-3 hours, depending on moisture in kernels. Drain off water. Spread wheat out. Air, oven, or dehydrator dry.

Kernels may be fried in a saucepan or in deep fat. For saucepan frying, use a small amount of oil. Stir kernels constantly. If you like crunchy nuts, fry longer than for soft nuts. Remove from fat with a slotted spoon. Drain. Season.

To deep fry, heat oil to 350-375°. Put kernels in a fine mesh sieve for easy removal. Cook to desired crunchiness. Drain. Season. Salt, seasoning, onion, garlic, barbecue or smoky salt all give a nice flavor. Grated Parmesan cheese is also good. Store, refrigerated, in an airtight container.

Wheat Pilaf

4 cups cooked wheat berries
1/4 cup butter
2 cups water

1 or 2 (4 oz.) cans drained mushrooms
Miso to taste

Sauté cooked wheat berries in butter for 5 to 10 minutes. Add Miso, mushrooms and water, stir. Cover. Simmer 1 to 3 hours. Extra liquid may be needed for long simmering.

Whole Wheat Casserole

3 cups cooked wheat berries
3 tablespoons butter
Miso to taste

1 cup water
1/2 cup chopped mushrooms

Brown cooked wheat berries in butter. Turn into a 1 1/2 quart casserole. Stir in Miso and 1 cup water. Bake in a 325° oven for 1 hour, checking occasionally to see if more liquid is needed. Add mushrooms; bake 15 minutes longer.

Wheat Coffee

Raw wheat berries

Coffee

Spread washed, dry wheat kernels on a cookie sheet. Bake in 350° oven for 1 hour. Run baked wheat through a coffee mill or grinder. Combine with regular coffee, half and half. This is best when brewed in a regular "perk" type pot.

Chapter One
What To Buy To Stock Your Pantry

Overnight (Insulated Jug) Wheat

3 cups water
$1^1/_3$ cups raw wheat

$^1/_2$ teaspoon salt
Insulated Bottle (Wide Mouth)

Put water, wheat and salt into a saucepan. Bring to a boil and simmer for 5 minutes. Pour the mixture into an insulated jug or bottle. Let stand for 8 hours or overnight.

The wheat berries are tender and ready to use; even hot, for a breakfast cereal. Use a wide mouth bottle or jug; it will be easier to get the wheat out.

Bulgar

Bulgar is made by soaking and cooking the whole wheat kernel, drying it and then removing part of the bran and cracking the remaining kernel into small pieces. It is man's oldest recorded use of wheat. Use it alone, mixed with fruits, vegetables, meats and salads. It can be boiled, roasted, fried and baked. Since bulgar is cooked in processing, it requires less time to cook than cracked wheat. It will double in volume when cooked and soaked in liquid.

Homemade Bulgar

1 cup whole wheat kernels (berries)   2 cups water

Combine wheat kernels and water in a saucepan. Cover; bring to a boil; simmer for 1 hour. Drain off any liquid remaining; it can be used in soups and gravies. Spread wheat out in a thin layer on a baking sheet. Bake for about 2 hours in a 200° oven or until completely dry. Leave the oven door open a crack so that moisture can escape. Crack the baked kernels in a mill or blender. Store in a dry, cool place.

Use in any recipe that calls for bulgar. To use: Boil in water for 5-10 minutes. It will almost double in volume. Bulgar is an excellent extender in meat loaves and casseroles. It is economical and adds a nice, nutlike flavor.

Cooked Wheat Berries

1 cup raw whole kernel wheat berries   5 cups water
$1/2$ teaspoon salt

You may cook the berries in one of four ways:
1. Soak raw wheat berries overnight (like beans). Drain water and add fresh water (3 cups) with $1/2$ teaspoon salt (opt.) and cook approximately 2 hours until tender.
2. Simmer above ingredients slowly over water in double boiler overnight at lowest temperature on your range.
3. Place all ingredients in a covered pan and bake about five hours or overnight in a warm oven (150-200°).
4. Rub slow cooker wall with 1 tablespoon butter. Cover the ingredients and cook on low for 8-9 hours.

Cook the wheat until tender. Drain well and cool. Cover; store in refrigerator or freeze for use in recipes (thaw before using). Makes about 3 cups.

"Montana Style" Wheat Chili

$1/2$ cup chopped green pepper $1/2$ cup chopped onion
1 8 oz. can tomato sauce   2 cups canned tomatoes
dash of paprika and cayenne   1 teaspoon salt
2 cups cooked wheat berries   2 teaspoons chili powder
olive oil

Sauté onions and green peppers in olive oil. Add remaining ingredients, cover and simmer one hour. Add water if needed.

Chapter One
What To Buy To Stock Your Pantry

A Kernel of Wheat

ENDOSPERM ... about 83% of the kernel
Source of white flour. Of the nutrients in the whole kernel the endosperm contains about:[1]
- 70-75% of the protein
- 43% of the pantothenic acid ⎫
- 32% of the riboflavin   ⎬ B-complex vitamins
- 12% of the niacin   ⎪
- 6% of the pyridoxine   ⎪
- 3% of the thiamine   ⎭

BRAN ... about 14½% of the kernel
Included in whole wheat flour but more often removed and used in animal or poultry feed. Of the nutrients in whole wheat, the bran, in addition to indigestible cellulose material contains about: [1]
- 86% of the niacin
- 73% of the pyridoxine
- 50% of the pantothenic acid
- 42% of the riboflavin
- 33% of the thiamine
- 19% of the protein

GERM ... about 2½% of the kernel
The embryo or sprouting section of the seed, usually separated because it contains fat which limits the keeping quality of flours. Available separately as human food, but usually added to animal or poultry feed.

Brown Rice Compared to Other Types of Rice

Composition of Rice (per 100 g or 3 oz))

	Brown Rice		White Rice			Enriched White Rice			Converted Rice (Enriched)		
1. Protein	7.5	g	6.7	g	90%	6.7	g	90%	7.4	g	99%
2. Minerals											
Calcium	32	mg	24	mg	75%	24	mg	75%	60	mg	190%
Phosphorous	221	mg	94	mg	43%	94	mg	43%	200	mg	90%
Iron	1.6	mg	0.8	mg	50%	2.9	mg	180%	2.9	mg	180%
Potassium	214	mg	92	mg	43%	92	mg	43%	50	mg	70%
Sodium	9	mg	5	mg	56%	5	mg	56%	9	mg	100%
3. Vitamins											
Thiamin	0.34	mg	0.07	mg	21%	0.44	mg	130%	0.44	mg	130%
Riboflavin	0.05	mg	0.03	mg	60%	0.03	mg	60%	0.03	mg	60%
Niacin	4.7	mg	1.6	mg	34%	3.5	mg	74%	3.5	mg	74%

Brown Rice

More rice is consumed in the world than any other grain. There's a good reason for this: rice is high in nutritional value. Although it's somewhat difficult to grow, billions of hard-working people throughout the world consider rice to be an imperative staple. And so will you once you enjoy it cooked in many different ways and benefit from its valuable minerals and vitamins.

Never buy white rice. The best part of its grain, the outer hull, has been polished away and used (hard to believe) to soak up oil on service station floors!

More on the uses of rice will follow, but be sure to try it steamed or boiled for breakfast with dates or raisins.

Oats

Oats are often thought of merely as oatmeal, but they have quite a lot going for them. First of all, they are usually quite inexpensive, especially when you buy a nice fat 100-pound sack of rolled oats at your feed store. (Won't it look reassuring in your pantry?) Nutritionally, brown rice and several other grains are more potent than oats, but just think of all the goodies you can make with a plentiful supply of oats: oatmeal cookies, with plenty of walnuts and perhaps some raisins, oatmeal pancakes, and tasty, economical meat loaves. Or how about some beautifully browned oatmeal bread or muffins, oatmeal cake and hot cherry pudding made with cherries you picked yourself in some farmer's orchard? So don't consider your pioneer pantry complete without an easy-to-store sack of oats.

Barley

Barley is one of the most neglected basic grains. There's no real reason for this; barley is a nutty-tasting, solid-bodied grain that can add a lot to your daily menu at extremely low cost. Canned-soup makers load their meat-based soups with it because they know it's cheap and richly flavored. But don't buy it manufactured into a high-priced item; just go down and pick up a sack or two for yourself.

Millet

"Me, eat bird seed?" That could be the plaintive cry of someone just introduced to this grain; most of us do associate it with bird-seed mix, and the little round grains do resemble something that a parakeet would love. What most people in America don't know is that millet, an easily grown staple, is an important and basic food to hundreds of millions of people worldwide. It's not the tastiest grain going, but it can be added to other foods to increase nutritional value. Your soups and stews will have more body and textural interest if you simply add a handful or so of millet before simmering. Millet is often cooked with stock and used as a side dish with fish or chicken. It even makes a fine candy; just cook it for a time with honey, pour it out to cool, and cut it into bars.

Corn

So highly regarded by the Aztecs that they often cast its image in solid gold, corn has always been and still is a world favorite. Buy it in whole-kernel form as shown here. In this way, it's undegerminated so you get full food value. You can make your own fresh cornmeal in your own blender. Stock up on corn; it's inexpensive and tasty.

Rye

Rye is best-known here as a main ingredient in bread, but it is a well-accepted grain in Europe, particularly in Russia. Many experts claim that dark bread made mainly from rye flour is far healthier than any other kind. Rye bread certainly has a distinctive and unique flavor and goes well with many robust, peasant-style dishes. Red cabbage demands a rye accompaniment. Rye may be purchased in whole-grain form or as ready-ground flour; either way it's a solid staple that should be in a well-stocked pantry.

Soybeans
Truly a wonder legume, the soybean is a must for any larder that combines high-quality nutrition with low cost. Soybeans are so important to any diet that a separate chapter is devoted to them later in this book. Soybeans will make a 99¢ per meal diet possible with money to spare.

The Chinese have had many thousands of years to develop a national diet, and even a philosophy of life, around soybeans. The amazing variety of dishes they make from soybeans will astound you unless you are already familiar with them. But rather than overstate our case in this brief introduction, turn to the soy chapter and see what a bonanza of good nutrition and good taste you'll find in soybeans and their related products.

Beans in General
Pinto, lima, red, kidney, great northern, and navy are but a few of the many varieties of delicious and nutritious beans. Beans vary in nutritional content, but they often make a fine substitute for the proteins found in meat. Further, they can be prepared in an infinite variety of ways. Beans are usually inexpensive, but their prices vary with availability. Become aware of price fluctuations. Simply wait out high prices and buy when the beans you want become reasonable again. Because they store well, buy a lot when the price is down; you'll feel a great sense of security with so much good food tucked away.

Split peas
Split peas are closely related to the bean family. They should definitely be considered an important part of your pioneer pantry. They're easily storable, nutritious, relatively inexpensive, and are always ready to go into the soup or stew pot to make a good dish

better. They're great alone too, simmered with lots of onions in the classic split-pea soup.

Potatoes

Potatoes rank next in line with the long-term storables such as grains and beans. They are much more valuable nutritionally than commonly believed and they're not even fattening if you go easy on the butter and sauces. These delicious tubers can be a mainstay to your diet; all they need is a chance to prove their merit through creative cooking. Spuds are important enough to warrant a chapter of their own.

Onions

Onions are a friendly companion to potatoes and lots of other good things. They should rank high on your priority list for staple items. Recent studies indicate that they are valuable in maintaining good health and preventing many types of nutritionally related disabilities, so eat lots of these fine, easily stored vegetables. There are virtually unlimited ways of preparing onions, from just plain sliced and raw to elegant French style onion soup with cheese and croutons.

There are dozens of varieties of onions: red, white, yellow, Bermuda, and green, to mention a few of the most popular. Major variance is in strength of flavor; the bigger onions, such as the large red ones, have a less pungent taste. Some of these are so mild that they can be eaten raw like apples. Yellow onions of medium size are probably the most commonly used in cooking. Green onions are flavorful and healthy; they can be added raw to salads or used as a garnish.

Peanut

Chapter One
What To Buy To Stock Your Pantry

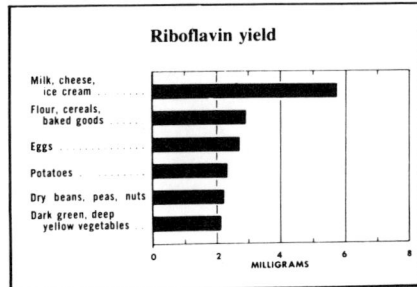

Garlic

This tasty bulb is a smaller, stronger relative of the onion. Long a standby of French and Italian cooks, you'll find it a most useful adjunct to basic food cookery. For example, added to rice pilaf (recipe later) garlic makes an otherwise bland food delicious.

Here are the most common ways of utilizing this flavorful and healthful food: For salads, peel and halve a clove of garlic and rub sides of wooden salad bowl, or simply soak a clove in your homemade oil and vinegar salad dressing. For spaghetti and macaroni sauces and similar dishes, peel, slice and sauté in butter. Then add other ingredients.

Shallots, a less strong relative of garlic, can be used in similar ways.

Cheese. An excellent source of protein.

Nuts. A source of protein plus fats, minerals, and vitamins.

Raw certified milk. Another high-protein food.

Vegetables. Organic and fresh vegetables provide almost everything needed for good health.

Chapter One
What To Buy To Stock Your Pantry

Fruits. Vitamin and mineral content alone make them a must for a healthy diet.

Eggs. Use only natural eggs from farm-raised (not assembly-line) chickens.

Seeds. They contain the best balance of nutrients in nature.

Sprouts. Even more nutritional value than seeds.

Honey. A natural sugar, but go easy.

Blackstrap molasses. Energy plus minerals; a natural sweet.

Wheat germ. The richest known source of Vitamin E.

Alfalfa. Very rich in minerals.

Bone meal. A good source of calcium and phosphorus.

Desiccated liver. Lots of B-12 plus other vitamins and minerals.

Brewer's yeast. Contains concentrated proteins.

Fish liver oils. Contains substantial amounts of Vitamins A and D.

Rose hips. Contain ten times the Vitamin C in other foods.

Kelp. An excellent source of trace minerals.

Meat. A good protein source if it's high-quality and pure.

Poultry. A protein source; again, avoid chemical birds.

Fish. Protein equal to that in meat and eggs; lots of phosphorus.

Natural vegetable oils. The real stuff contains valuable blood components.

Herb teas. Fine home remedies for what ails you.

Yogurt. Easily digested; high in vitamins.

Vitamin Supplements. Use as needed, but only from natural sources.

Soybeans. Rank with meat, milk, fish and eggs, as a protein source.

Raw juices. Great substitutes for coffee and tea.

Chapter Two

Where To Shop And

How To Do It

**What You'll Learn:
Alternatives to supermarkets — wholesale grocers, natural food stores, feed stores, and produce markets — and how to use them.**

Recently, on a family outing my wife went into a supermarket to buy some food for lunch. When she returned empty-handed a few minutes later, I asked her why. "Everything in that store was wrapped in plastic. Two slices of phony meat loaded with preservatives for 89 cents! I just couldn't bear to waste our money on it." This incident left a profound impression on us. It made us realize that it's becoming less and less possible to buy something

— anything — in a conventional grocery store that's worth buying, let alone worth *eating*. Consumers are bearing the brunt of this trend more heavily every day. Artificial, heavily processed non-food sealed in plastic or metal is junk for robots, not people. But there are ways to avoid the food-for-profit conspiracy.

First of all, make sure you know the meaning of the following terms:

Cooperative Buying: Two or more people pool their money and buy as a group. They share in accordance with their contributions of money and time.

Wholesale Buying: Buying at grocers' prices. Sometimes the discounts are substantial; at other times they are minimal but still worth the effort.

Bulk Buying: Buying in large quantities. Not necessarily wholesale buying, since many retail sales are made in bulk quantities; for example, you can buy a 100 pound sack of whole grain wheat at many feed stores or grain mills, and outlets are opening up advertising "survival foods" in bulk quantities.

In Berkeley, California, two families I know occupy two separate floors of a huge, old-fashioned house. One is the family of an engineer and one of an attorney. These people are well-educated and have learned to apply their intelligence and training to the problem of high food costs. First, they pooled their grocery money. Second, they went to a local wholesale grocer; that is, the grocer who provides staple foods to small "Mom and Pop" grocery stores. The small store grocer comes in regularly to buy a sack of this, a half a case of that, a wheel or two of cheese, etc. The terms are usually cash on the proverbial barrelhead. The attorney and engineer told the wholesale grocer that they, too, would like to buy wholesale. Since they agreed to abide by the cash terms, the wholesaler was pleased to cooperate. The families now buy canned vegetables by the case for a substantial percentage less than individual shelf prices. They buy 100 pound sacks of dried beans, brown rice, potatoes, onions, and other basic staples such as wheels of cheese and spices in bulk. The big house has a large

Chapter Two
Where To Shop And How To Do It

storage room or pantry and this has begun to look like a wholesale grocery facility itself! Just think of the savings these families are making! They buy cooperatively and in quantity and share the purchases equally. For example, by purchasing powdered milk in 100 pound sacks, they have driven the cost down to less than 50 percent of the boxed price. By purchasing cheese in wheels and cutting and wrapping it into individual portions themselves, they pay about 70 percent less than the retail price for this important protein source. During periods when foods are abundant due to seasonal harvest, they buy boxes of apples and pears, lugs of tomatoes and peppers, and sacks of staples such as sweet potatoes and popcorn. On every possible occasion the families join forces and go into the nearby rural areas to pick fruit and nuts direct from the farmers' trees.

It's apparent that by buying cooperatively in bulk quantities and at wholesale prices this team has discovered a way to save thousands of dollars a year! In the process, they have learned two things: (1) It's fun for the whole family (children love to play grocer, cutting and wrapping cheese and drying fruits on the roof); and (2) Everyone becomes more skillful with experience. Bargaining becomes sharper when you've had a few sessions behind you.

In summary, we suggest that you consider all three aspects of this method, cooperative, wholesale, and bulk buying. However, if for any reason you can't manage all three, then at least try one or two. A single person, for example, can buy in reasonably large bulk quantities. And single people can join the cooperative food groups springing up in great numbers all over America. Check with your local natural food store or community action groups for co-ops in your area. If you don't find one, think about starting one of your own.

Wholesale grocers often require a resale permit number, which is what you obtain when you take out a license to operate a business in some states. If you run up against this requirement, try to find someone who has a relative or friend with such a resale permit number that he would be willing to let your group use from time to time. If all else fails, you could even start up a small grocery store of your own. Many people have done this. Business licenses aren't too expensive, and a tiny hole-in-the-wall grocery can actually return enough profit to pay more than its expenses. Thus you would have an unlimited source of food at wholesale prices. Here's an area in which your resourcefulness and ingenuity will pay off in big returns.

Natural Food Stores

These quaint places are springing up everywhere. They are usually manned by aware people who are more interested in selling nutritious food than making a profit. If you've never been in one, you have a pleasant surprise in store. First, they're usually relaxed and imaginatively decorated, and there's a feeling of, "O.K., let's have some fun while we're shopping and talking about healthful food."

The shopkeepers, men or women, are usually healthy and energetic; after all, they eat what they sell. Ask them what to buy. They'll know which items are particularly plentiful at the time, which ones will make up a special-company meal, and which foods to buy for more energy.

Chapter Two
Where To Shop And How To Do It

Speaking of energy foods, you'll find big bins of natural grains — wheat, rice, oats, barley, millet, and corn. This is the place to stock your pantry. The store may have a grinder, hand or electric, so you can fresh-grind your purchase.

And for the best tasting and most nutritious peanut butter you'll ever eat, trying grinding your own from fresh raw peanuts in most any natural food store. Surprisingly, it's cheaper than supermarket commercial brands.

Look up your nearest natural food outlet under "Natural," "Health," "Organic," or similar listings in the phone book yellow pages. Avoid stores that only carry elaborately packaged items such as bottles of vitamins and over-priced, over-processed cereals. Health food stores have been known to play the food-for-profit game as well as supermarkets. Write to *Prevention* Magazine, 33 East Minor Street, Emmaus, PA 18049, for a list of good stores.

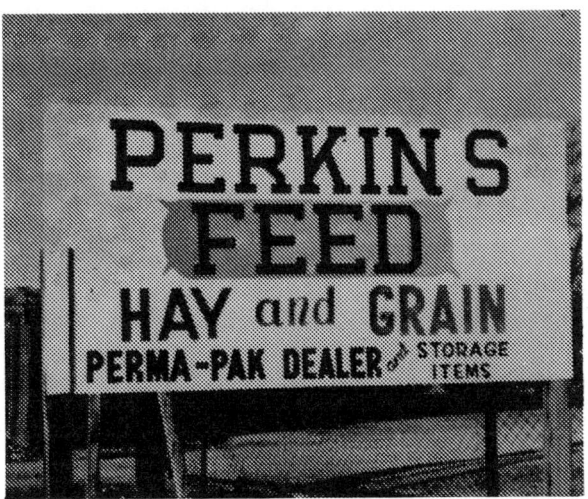

Feed Stores

I grew up thinking that a feed store was for animals exclusively. Then one day I noticed that the whole wheat I had purchased for my horses looked both appealing and nutritious. If good old Pixie, my quarter horse mare, thrived on it, why couldn't we? I took a small amount home and put it through my old-fashioned meat grinder, fine blade. Suddenly it resembled something that I knew well, a packaged hot cereal made from wheat. Hey, I thought, have I been...? Yes, I was paying a lot more for the grocery-store version of wheat cereal than I should have been — eight times more, as a matter of fact.

From this day on, I shared all kinds of grains with gentle Pixie. I found that the feed store I went to could obtain every grain imaginable — oats, rice, corn, millet, barley, plus all kinds of seeds (sunflower, alfalfa, sesame), and beans, peanuts, and wheat germ. In short, the feed store could provide anything in the basic bulk, unpackaged line. And prices? Lower than I'd ever thought possible. At that time, in 1969, sacks of rolled oats that would last my family for months cost three or four dollars. Now they average about $35, which is still a bargain, considering skyrocketing supermarket prices. Wheat germ, fresh from the mill was about 15 cents a pound in paper sacks. (Compare that to what you pay for a glass jar of wheat germ in your local supermarket.)

I began saving so much money, I thought there must be a Catch 22 in it somewhere. So I asked the feed store manager about purity. He said, "Bill, if we sold anything that would harm the race horses that eat our products, we'd be out of business in a month." Realizing that I was insured for a lot less than the race horse in the pasture adjoining Pixie's, I stopped worrying.

Of course, there's always a possibility that what you buy there may not be suitable for human consumption without some processing; oats need to be rolled and hulled, for example. But for the most part, everything in a feed and grain store is ready to use. To get you started, here's a recipe that will provide you with a low-cost, natural and healthful breakfast tomorrow morning if you pick up a sack of whole grain wheat at your local feed store today.

Grind the wheat in your old meat grinder or use the blender at high speed. Boil a pint of water; add salt if you wish. Slowly add the fresh-ground wheat, about 4 to 6 ounces depending on whether you want your cereal thin or thick. Stir. Turn down the heat and let it

Chapter Two
Where To Shop And How To Do It

bubble for 10 to 15 minutes with an occasional stir. If desired, add some chopped dates, nuts, or snipped-up dried fruit just before removing from stove.

Voilà! You have two large bowls of fresh ground cereal complete with the original wheat germ. Add some milk or cream, a spoonful of honey, and sit down to a great natural breakfast. Costs? Aside from the things you added, about 14 cents for two half-pound bowls! Compare that 7 cent breakfast of steaming whole wheat with a bowl of pallid, over-priced and over-sugared packaged cereal and draw your own conclusions.

You'll find natural grains in bulk form in stores listed under "Feed," "Hay," "Grain," "Ranch" or "Farm" in the yellow pages.

Produce Markets

When I was a small boy, the Great Depression was in full swing. "No Help Wanted" signs festooned the stores and shops of the small town, South Pasadena, California, where I lived. My family wasn't poverty-stricken, but low-cost or no-cost food was always welcome. I quickly learned that there was lots of fine food behind grocery stores. For example, the green grocer would peel off a few leaves from each head of lettuce every day to give them a fresh appearance. Once the heads had been reduced to small cannonball size, they were tossed in the out basket. Think of it! Heads of lettuce for free! After frequenting the backs of stores for a while, I became more sophisticated. I would arrive on the scene just as the store was closing for the day. I'd offer to haul away anything that was going to be tossed out. Many fine, only slightly broken watermelons and only lightly dappled apples made their way into my little red wagon. With a bit of deft surgery, they became every bit as good as the produce selling at full price.

A variation on this theme brings us into the big time. Start haunting the major wholesale produce markets in larger towns and cities. Often you can get whole crates of unsold, slightly over-ripe fruits and vegetables for free or a fraction of their original wholesale price, which is low to begin with. Not too long ago I picked up a crate of tangelos (like oranges only larger) which were considered defective because they were dark-skinned (the taste was unaffected). The cost? The labor it took to get them into my car's trunk.

Ranches, Farms, and Roadside Stands

Combine a delightful picnic or nature-study trip with a good food hunting expedition. You'll enjoy yourself, you'll save money, and you'll drive home with a car full of the freshest food possible. Roadside stands provide the easiest, most convenient access to

Chapter Two
Where To Shop And How To Do It

farm-fresh produce. But many farms don't have stands, yet are still interested in making cash sales. So don't hesitate to drive into a likely looking orchard or field. Barter a bit with the owner and you may end up with a trunk full of off-the-stalk corn or ripe-from-the-tree peaches.

VISIT THE FARM

**PRODUCE, HOUSEPLANTS, NURSERY, ANTIQUES
SPECIALTY GIFTS, QUILTS**

Walnuts 35¢ lb., 3 lbs. - $1.00
Avocados 20¢ each
FRESH PICKED ORGANIC PRODUCE

5555 Soquel — halfway between Cabrillo & Soquel Village

Another way to find rural food bargains is to buy the local town or county paper, often a weekly with ads offering "Fresh, picked organic produce," "Fresh ground wheat & corn meal, etc."

What if you buy too much? Learn how to preserve the surplus upcoming. Or barter the extra apples for staples at your natural food store. Or just be generous; share your largesse with the less fortunate. Incidentally, as you will note in the ad, some farmers are willing to let you pick your own and charge accordingly, usually very little. If you've never done this, you have a most pleasant experience in store. You can make it an impromptu party amidst the trees. And remember, the few fruits you eat don't get counted (but don't worry, the farmer makes allowances for picker consumption). Once you try it, you'll find that no plum, peach, apricot or cherry ever tasted as good as the one you picked yourself. The fruit will be sun-warm and fully ripe. Plucking them from a leafy tree in some verdant orchard on a beautiful afternoon in late August will stay in your memory and draw you back year after year.

I've already just begun here to hint at the opportunities for acquiring your food in alternative stores and rural regions. There are fish farms, dairies, cheese factories, dried-fruit barns, vineyards and many other food-preparation facilities dotted throughout the U.S. countryside. Many sell to travelers as part of their regular business. Others can be persuaded to part with a crate of peaches, a wheel of cheese, for money or the right barter item. So think of this brief review as a beginner's guide. Take it from here yourself.

Chapter Three

How To Develop Your

Bargaining Skills

What You'll Learn:

That you can take advantage of the law of supply and demand, even to the extent of naming your own price.

Since this book was written, the distinction between organically grown fruits and veggies and the ordinary, chemically-treated kind has become quite clear and noteworthy. Use every opportunity to avoid the latter. Your health comes first!

It's a well-known and lamentable fact that hundreds of tons of perfectly good food are thrown away each day in the United States simply because we are a rich nation (at least at this time) and care little for the losses that accrue from this wasteful practice. But you can take advantage of the general wastefulness by becoming a weekend warrior, mounting regular attacks on the bargain counters.

Don't try this if you're the fussy type (and I don't think you are or you wouldn't be reading this book). Keep an open mind and a ready purse; you never know when you'll spot a bargain. Don't hesitate to buy too much at one time; you can use surplus foods to barter for other things with your neighbors or with other merchants. Also, modern techniques of preserving allow you to store perishables for long periods of time.

Try these bargain-hunting techniques the next time you go shopping. Simply follow the rule that prices are determined by the law of supply and demand. Concentrate on items that are in great supply but have little demand, and learn to be in the right place at the right time.

Bargaining for Produce

If you live near a food market that closes on Sunday, drop in and have a chat with the manager some late Saturday evening just before closing. Tell him that you are a regular customer and that you are interested in helping him by buying items that are not up to selling standards but which are still edible and wholesome. For example, it's hard to sell an apple that has a worm hole or soft spot in it. Such items are usually left at the end of the week's sale. No one wants them when a perfect apple is available for the same price. But there's nothing wrong with an apple of this type that a paring knife can't cure in about two seconds. Cut out the worm hole or soft spot and the apple is as perfect as one selling for full price. The same is true of cantaloupes, watermelons, avocados, or pears that have an overripe spot. Simply cut around the spot and eat all the rest.

In the case of vegetables, make sure that despite the damaged spot the produce is still fairly fresh. Old, limp, tired and wilted vegetables have lost so much of their vitamins that they are simply not worth buying. Winter vegetables such as cabbages, cauliflower, beets, turnips, rutabagas, potatoes and onions are not

Chapter Three
How To Develop Your Bargaining Skills

quite as delicate as other vegetables, though. These have a somewhat longer life and will store fairly well if kept in a cool, dry place.

So, if you come across some damaged but still fairly fresh-appearing fruits or vegetables at your neighborhood market, your task is to buy them for as little as you can. Remember that the grocer doesn't necessarily waste this food; he takes it home and eats it himself. He is not about to give it away if he can sell it. But when stocks are plentiful, the chances are he will be willing to sell for very little. This is where your bargaining abilities can be put to good use. It's quite certain that you and the grocer can come to an agreement on a fair price for items that must be sold for cash immediately. Once you have established rapport, it will be simple for you to do most of your fruit and vegetable shopping at the end of the week. If you should latch onto a whole lug box of soft peaches, make peach jam. If you come across some overripe tomatoes, boil them tender and chuck them into your blender for instant tomato sauce, then freeze or bottle. Perhaps you can acquire a large quantity of oranges with dry, hard skins. These are hard to sell, but they're great for juice. Squeeze them and freeze the juice you can't drink immediately.

Once you've developed your bargaining skills, start using your imagination. Consider any business that deals in good food fair game. Harry and David, for instance, is the firm that started the Fruit of the Month Club. Based in Medford, Oregon, they send gift packages of fresh fruits to all parts of the world. Their high-quality gift boxes contain only the most perfect specimens of the superlative fruit grown in their orchards. Thus, after their seasonal packaging of such items as peaches and pears, you can visit their plant in Medford and purchase large bags of what they term "rejects" for very little money. Actually, their "rejects" would outshine the best fruit in many high-class markets, since many pears are rejected, for instance, only because they are too big to conform to the standards set for gift packages.

Check around your own city and the surrounding countryside to see if there isn't a dairy, chicken farm, potato processor, or other food-handling facility that would be willing to sell you their off-standard items at a low price.

Variations on the Theme

This bargaining technique can be applied to many other types of stores: bakeries, meat markets, fish and seafood shops and dairies. Many bakeries, for example, will not hold products over a weekend. If you approach a baker late on Saturday, you may find an opportunity to stock your freezer with low-cost baked goods for perhaps half their regular retail price.

Fish and seafood shops are especially vulnerable to sharp bargains. Fish has notoriously poor keeping qualities. Thus, you might make an agreement with your local fish merchant to take anything off his hands that is approaching unsalability. What can you do with a fish that will only last another day? Well, you can cut it up and freeze it, make it into a bouillabaisse and freeze it, or smoke and save it for an almost indefinite time in your refrigerator.

Bargaining for Fresh Food

Be on the lookout for a farmer, rancher, or truck gardener who could use some help. Offer to provide labor in exchange for fresh-pulled carrots, beets, cabbages, and lettuce. My wife Ruth wrote this to me recently: "Helped Ms. Webb pick a lug of cukes for a customer and she gave me plums, apples, squash, cukes and a gallon of milk." While you'd be lucky to run into a cornucopia like that, the thought is worth keeping in mind whenever you're out for a drive.

Chapter Four

Where To Pick

Fresh Foods For Free

What You'll Learn:

How to find the thousands of sources of free foods throughout the United States.

A sparkling day, a melodious brook, trees festooned with climbing flowers — a perfect time for a picnic. Perhaps on such a day you discovered foods that you could have for the picking. It may have been watercress, the crisp, tart plant that grows wild in many streams. Or it may have been the sweet wild blackberries that grow in abundance in many parts of the country. It could have been the black walnut that grows wild and produces some of the tastiest nut tidbits in the world. These are just three of the thousands of wild foods that you can gather up free of cost. The world is still full of good things to eat; it's a matter of keeping your eyes open.

Cattails

This prolific plant, which grows in most swamp and marsh areas of the world, is a treasure trove of delicious tidbits. I discovered this for myself one afternoon in the Santa Ynez river valley behind Santa Barbara. I had been swimming in a wonderful swimming hole, a place where the river slowed, widened, and deepened beneath a rocky bluff. On the opposite side, a gently sloping sandy beach was partly covered by a thick growth of cattails — tall, green and lush. While swimming underwater, I could see white tendrils growing out of the cattail roots. I snapped off a couple and, willing to try anything once, surfaced and ate them. Wonderful! They tasted like the tenderest hearts of celery I'd ever had. That day I ate almost every cattail tendril I could find. I felt as though I had made a great discovery. What I didn't know was that the Chumash Indians, who once lived in that region, thought that cattail tendrils were just about as basic as the acorns they also used as a staple.

Later, when I read books on survival and life in the wilderness, I discovered that almost all parts of the cattail are useful — from the tendrils to the seed pod. The roots are the most basic edible

Chapter Four
Where To Pick Fresh Foods For Free

part of the plant. Next in importance are the new shoots; you'll find these in abundance. Peel and eat them as you would fresh tender celery. Finally, try the yellow pollen produced by the seed pods. It can be used as flour if you gather enough, or added to soups, stews, cereals or anything you wish, for bulk and nutrition.

The Homely But Tasty Cactus

Stands of thorny cactus abound in the western deserts and desert rims. They look unapproachable, but the common, broad-leafed cactus is eaten by thousands of people daily. Almost all the other North American cacti are edible and can be sliced and fried, boiled, roasted, or added to stews and soups.

Here's the procedure. Wear gloves and use a large knife or machete to cut off slabs of cactus leaves. Then fill a tub or bucket with water. Submerge the cactus and using a small paring knife dig out the clusters of sharp spines. These will float to the surface where they can be skimmed off. The spines can also be burned off over a gas flame or campfire.

Just for fun, here's one recipe. It should trigger your imagination and encourage you to experiment.

Nopales, Basic Preparation

After you make sure all the prickly spines are removed, cut the cactus leaves into cubes. Boil in slightly salted water until tender. Eat with butter, salt and pepper as a vegetable, chill and add to salads, or pickle. Any way you try them, they're not only good, they're free!

Smell Them First, Then Eat Them

I'm talking about wild roses. They are an excellent source of Vitamin C and it's yours for the taking. The vitamin is contained in the buds, or "rose hips," of wild and domestic roses. These edible goodies are the red-orange, smooth-skinned berries that grow at the end of the rose stem. They taste like apples (to which they are related). You can gather them to eat on the trail or take them home and prepare them in a number of ways. They can actually be used as if they were small apples. Incidentally, in Scandinavian countries rose hips are dried and powdered. The powder is used in fruit soups and hot or cold drinks, on cereals, and wherever else a sweet, nutritious powdered substance is called for. Here's a good way to put rose hips to work for you.

Rose Hip Jam

Cut the rose hips in half and remove the seeds. Chop or grind the hips and add four cups to about 2 cups of water. Boil for about ½ hour. Then add as much raw sugar or honey as you wish and continue boiling until it reaches the desired thickness. Somewhere along the way, remove some and use it as rose hip syrup on pancakes, waffles, and biscuits. When the jam is thick, remove from fire, pour into sterilized jars, and seal in the conventional way. If you wish, add a little cinnamon or lemon juice for more flavor.

Piñon Nuts

These tasty and nutritious nuts are found in the cones of the piñon tree, a short, snarled pine of the southwest. Gathering them can be fun if you make sure to take some solvent along to dissolve the sticky sap that accompanies the cone.

Piñon nuts are sold in many places as alternatives to peanuts though their flavor is really more delicate. Piñon nuts can also be ground into flour. Removed from their soft shell and pounded, they become a wonderful addition to pancake batter, cookies, or other baked goods. Try sprinkling a few shelled nuts on top of plain cookies.

Piñon

Birch

Birch Tea

Birch trees abound in North America. Most people remember their tall beauty and some know that the bark can be used as canoe material. But few people are aware that birches can provide a most refreshing tea. Just gather young leaves, bark, and the soft new growth between the wood and bark. Chop it up and boil it in water. It becomes a most delicious beverage with a flavor similar to that of wintergreen tea.

Birches have other uses too. The young, tender, inner bark can be eaten raw, cut into strips and added to stews or soups, or dried and carried for munching on the trail. The sap of birches can be gathered and boiled for use as a delicately flavored syrup. Drill a small hole in the tree in spring or early summer when the sap is flowing best. Hang a small tin can or cup beneath the hole and go on to the next tree while the first one drips. When you've collected a substantial amount of sap, boil it until it reaches the desired thickness, add a speck of cinnamon or other spice, and you have an unusually tasty syrup for just the fun of making it.

Blackberries

Of all the berries that grow wild in the North American continent, none is so sweet, so lush, and so easy to find as the blackberry. Bushes of these luscious treats grow alongside roads and byways in many states. In terms of time expended, little compares with the returns from a berry-picking expedition. Besides the obvious and instant pleasure of eating them right off the bush, there are dozens of ways to make wild blackberries a part of your gourmet diet. Here are just a few:

Blackberry Slump (Cobbler)

4 cups blackberries
4 tablespoons cornstarch
1 teaspoon nutmeg

$1/2$ cup honey (optional if berries are sweet enough for your taste)

Chapter Four
Where To Pick Fresh Foods For Free

Bring these slowly to a boil in a heavy saucepan. While the mixture is simmering, make a batter of:

2 tablespoons honey
$1/2$ cup milk
$1^1/2$ teaspoons baking powder

3 tablespoons shortening
$1^1/2$ cups sifted whole wheat flour

Cream honey and shortening. Add the milk and mix thoroughly. Sift the flour and baking powder together. Stir rapidly into the other ingredients. Then begin dropping the batter, spoonful by spoonful, over the bubbling berries. Cover and cook at the same speed for 10 minutes. Serve hot with cream.

Blackberry Pie

This pie isn't solid with thickeners such as arrowroot, tapioca, or cornstarch, so it won't hold together while you punctuate your conversation with the occasional forkful. As a matter of fact, most backwoodsmen who sit down to this particular dessert are glad to hold up on the repartee for a while and finish off with a spoon.

Blackberry bramble

All you need besides the pastry is 4 cups of fresh blackberries, $1/2$ cup honey, and $3/4$ cup melted butter. As for the cooking, it just takes a single operation.

Line well-greased pie pan with pastry. Mix the berries, honey, and butter. Pour them into the uncooked shell. Top with the upper crust, making sure to cut vents. Bake in a preheated oven at 375° for about 50 minutes or until the crust is golden brown.

Blackberry Jam

Boil together for 5 minutes: 4 cups blackberries, 1 cup honey, and 1 teaspoon mixed cloves, cinnamon, and nutmeg. Remove from heat and add a bottle of commercial pectin. Skim, pour into sterile jars, seal, label, and store.

Acorns

Common oak

Acorns were once a staple of many Indian groups, and are still eaten in many parts of the world. These oak nuts are nutritious and tasty. All they need is preliminary treatment to remove tannin. Just grind them up and leach the tannin out with changes of hot water. Or simply boil them for a while, then dry and grind them into flour. Use as you would any coarse whole wheat flour. Indians made cakes similar to pancakes or tortillas from acorn flour.

Olives

Las Vegas, Nevada would probably be the last place you would think to look for wild or free food. But down the street from where I'm writing these words dozens of olive trees are thriving. At this time of year, late fall, they are laden with hundreds of pounds of ripening olives, and no one seems to want the fruit, including the owners of the trees. The olives drop to the ground on the neighborhood lawns and rot. Some enterprising soul could make a seasonal habit to knock on doors and get permission to pick the olives. After all, olives are one of the few fruits or vegetables that produce a large quantity of usable oil.

Fishing

Many astute food gatherers carry a small, compact fishing pole or drop line in their cars or jacket pockets. It's a good habit to develop. Whenever you spot a likely place to drop a line, do it. A fat, fresh fish might grace your frying pan that very evening. A small slingshot or small air pistol can serve to bag you some small animals.

This chapter has only scratched the surface of what's available to you practically in your own back yard. The U.S. Army *Survival Guide* (this is a small sampling of the thousands of wild foods that you can gather up free of cost) notes that 300,000 plants grow on our planet, and that over 100,000 are edible. So expand your food horizons; not all of what you eat need come from a store. And think of the outdoor exercise you'll get while toting your market basket through wood and glade!

Eat Well For 99¢ A Meal

Foraged Foods

Chapter Five

Your Kitchen

Is Your Workshop

> **What You'll Learn:**
> How the right tools can make cooking
> for you and your family a great pleasure.

You really need very few items to set up a basic working kitchen: a convenient place to chop and cut, a pot, a pan, a good knife, a wooden spoon perhaps, and a pancake turner. A strainer is handy too. Remember what great food you can make in the wilds with nothing but a few green sticks and some know-how. Buy your kitchen utensils as you find them at flea markets, the Salvation Army, or garage sales. And restaurant-supply houses are great places to browse in when you're out to stock your kitchen. To get you thinking, an inventory is given below. No one needs all this junk, but it will let you know what's available.

Basic Necessities
Pans
    1-quart with lid
    3-quart with lid
    2- or 3-quart double boiler

Skillets
    6-inch with lid
    10-inch with lid

Kettles
    6-quart with lid

Baking pans
    6-quart dutch oven
    15-inch pan
    13 x 9 x 2-inch cake pan
    9 x 5 x 3-inch loaf pan (several)
    2 cookie sheets
    muffin pan

Casseroles and Bowls
    2-quart casserole with lid
    nest of mixing bowls

Measurers
    measuring spoon cluster
    2 4-cup liquid measuring cups
    graduated dry measuring cups cluster

Thermometers
    meat, deep fat, and oven

Cutlery
    2 paring knives
    all-purpose medium-size knife
    large slicing knife
    vegetable peeler
    cleavers, one small, one large
    grater
    food grinder
    kitchen shears
    sharpening stone or knife sharpener

Other Utensils
    wooden spoons, assorted sizes and shapes
    ladle
    cooking fork
    strainer
    funnel
    pancake turner
    egg beater
    fruit juicer
    corkscrew
    can and bottle opener

You'll determine your needs based on this list depending on how much you like tools for their own sake and how well you can

Chapter Five
Your Kitchen Is Your Workshop

adapt one tool to a variety of purposes. Now on to the more exotic possibilities.

The Fireless Cooker

When I was a small boy, my father often took me to barbecues sponsored by his company. These were Spanish-style outings where whole sides of beef would be placed over glowing coals in a huge pit, covered tightly, and allowed to mellow slowly throughout the long day. I've never forgotten the taste of those tender succulent morsels of beef, and I've never been able to describe it. Often, beans and potatoes were cooked in the pit, too, and they were equally delicious. You can achieve these ambrosial results in your own home; all you need to do is build yourself a simple fireless cooker.

The fireless cooker consists of a cooking pot tightly sealed within an insulated box. Start with a Dutch oven, the heavy cast iron type, and find a large pasteboard, wooden, or metal box big enough to contain it. Place lots of crumpled newspapers in the bottom of the box, put the oven

Fireless cookers

Save Your Time, Money and Food
By Cooking With a "Best Made" Fireless Cooker!

$9.85

STEAM TIGHT COVER
ALUMINUM LINED
THROUGHOUT

Single Compartment
All you have to do is heat the food to boiling point in one of the aluminum vessels and place inside the aluminum lined compartment with hot soapstones. They hold enough heat to cook an entire meal. The compartments are insulated throughout and fitted with steamtight covers. Especially useful on auto trips, picnics, etc.

on them and then tightly pack newspapers all around the sides to fill the remaining space in the box. It's that simple, although you might want to add a few personal refinements. Professionally built fireless cookers consist of smooth-sided tubes into which the cooking pot fits. They also have handy lids to seal off the pot. But the homemade version works on the same principle. All you're really after is a cooking container that retains its own heat.

To use the cooker, merely put the beans, or whatever you are going to cook, in the pot with all spices, water, and vegetables. Cover and bring to a boil on your regular stove. Then place the whole works in the insulated box, seal it up, and leave it for about eight hours. You can actually leave it overnight or for the day when you're going out and about. When you open the box you'll find that your meal has been cooked slowly in its own juices by the stored heat. What a grand meal to come home to!

The Blender
My wife says if she had to give up all her small appliances, her blender would be the last to go. She uses it for almost every meal. She throws in dried-out crusts of bread that accumulate to make bread crumbs. For nourishing drinks she tosses in any variety of fruit — an apple, a slightly overripe banana or peach, some leftover strawberries. To this she adds some skim milk, a bit of honey for sweetening, a raw egg yolk for protein, some wheat germ, and voilà! a complete and delicious lunch. An economical and swiftly made salad dressing will consist of some buttermilk, yogurt, mayonnaise and a hunk of blue cheese — a difficult mixture to make by hand but easy in the blender. And speaking of mayonnaise, we make our own in the blender and like it far better than any commercial variety. If you buy oil in bulk quantities, homemade mayonnaise costs far less than commercial brands.

The Yogurt Maker
If you're a yogurt enthusiast you may consider buying a yogurt maker, or you may be satisfied with a home-built set-up. The commercial yogurt maker consists mainly of a heat source and comes with its own jars, but you can get away with as little as one

Chapter Five
Your Kitchen Is Your Workshop

large jar as long as you can set it in a place which will give it some steady warmth. You can place the jar over the pilot on your stove or on a heating pad. Or perhaps you have a warm closet that houses the hot water heater.

Yogurt is one of those dishes that fits in anywhere. It's a meal in itself for those who prefer a light lunch, and a luxurious dessert for dinner if it's mixed with naturally sweet fruit. And so easy to make:

Homemade yogurt incubator

Yogurt

Mix 1 cup whole milk, 2 tablespoons commercial yogurt or yogurt from your last homemade batch, 1 cup non-instant milk powder, 3 cups warm water. Shake or blend. Pour mixture into small bowls and keep at about 110° F for 3 to 8 hours until set. When thick refrigerate. Flavor to suit with anything you like, from cinnamon to chopped fruits.

Chinese Items: Cleavers and Woks

The next time you go to a Chinese restaurant, ask the proprietor to let you tour the kitchen. There you'll see the Chinese secret to simple, efficient food preparation. There will be a sturdy chopping block, one end of which empties onto a work table, the other into a waste receptacle. Arranged nearby will be an assortment of high-carbon steel cleavers with edges like razors.

These relatively heavy cutting instruments make the chopping, slicing, dicing, and trimming of vegetables a pleasure. Try it yourself and see. The cleaver does all the work; you just raise it and lower it and keep your fingers out of the way. Once you're familiar with the cleaver, you won't want to go back to an ordinary knife. Since the Chinese use large quantities of vegetables in their cooking, it's understandable that they settled on a sturdy block and cleaver many centuries ago. If you have vegetarian leanings, you'll want to use that combination too.

The basic Chinese cooking utensil is the wok. It's a very simple, shallow metal bowl with sloping sides. Food is cooked at the center of the wok balanced over the heat source. Very little heat is required to cook foods in this way, an important consideration in fuel-poor areas of rural China and in energy-conscious American cities. Also, the edges of the wok retain heat, keeping the cooked, ready-to-serve foods warm once they leave the stove.

You'll find cleavers and woks in any Chinatown supply store. Or, if you're far from metropolitan areas, write the Chamber of Commerce in your closest major city and ask for up-to-date listings of suppliers.

From Wok to Crock

A large ceramic crock holding five gallons or more will be a valuable addition to your kitchen equipment. Heavy, durable, and big enough to stay put when you stir things in it, this container can be used in many ways. For example, it's the perfect place to mix your bread dough and let it rise. It's great for making batches of fruit drinks. And you can crush grapes or other fruits or do your pickling in it. When not in use for mixing, a crock is a fine place to store bulk foods.

The Witch's Cauldron

A companion to the ceramic crock is a big substantial pot. Restaurant kitchens, you'll find, always have a huge pot simmering on the back of the stove full of stock for soups, gravy or sauce.

Chapter Five
Your Kitchen Is Your Workshop

You'll need an oversized pot in which to make large quantities of chili beans, spaghetti sauce, clam chowder, or beef stew. Made at one time in quantity, these foods can be divided into meal-sized portions and frozen. Cooking in large quantities is one of the keys to cutting food costs.

The Tenderizer and The Masher
Among the smaller kitchen tools you'll need are the meat tenderizer (a hammer with a diamond pattern on its pounding surface), and a business-like potato masher. The latter is great for preparing the many dishes where reduction of ingredients to fine particles is essential.

Coffee Grinders

Coffee grinders are useful for many foods besides coffee: use one to make bean flour, blend dry ingredients when even distribution is essential, grind nuts into a flavorful powder, etc. You can often find grinders in antique stores, second-hand shops, and flea markets.

Coffee grinder

Meat grinder

Corn mill

To use the grinder efficiently, find a space on a sturdy bench, table, or sideboard where you can clamp it semi-permanently. Then it will always be ready when you need it.

Grain Grinders

Grain grinders are even more essential to the budget-conscious cook, but they are just as important in terms of nutrition. The old stone and flour mills our forefathers used produced flours and meal that retained all the important elements of each grain of wheat and each kernel of corn, including the vital germ oils. There was no heat problem during milling to cause the food to turn rancid and spoil, and there were no processing problems resulting in large losses of vital nutrients. With all the nourishing and tasty elements of the grain intact, breads, biscuits, pies, cakes, and other baked goods tasted great and were positive additions to a healthy diet. You can produce the same results straight from your pantry if you own your own hand- or motor-driven grain and flour mill. Many varieties are on the market. As an added bonus, you'll save a great deal of money in

Chapter Five
Your Kitchen Is Your Workshop
57

grinding your own flour. After all, when you buy packaged flour and meal, all you're really paying for is the labor and packaging.

Praise for The Oskar

Several years ago, Sunbeam gambled that people would buy a small food processor which they called the Oskar. They were right and we were one of their happiest customers. The unit makes food preparation a delight. For example, you can chop raw cabbage for cole slaw in seconds.

We've found that we eat lots more raw veggies because the Oskar takes all the work out of the preparation.

Chapter Six

Food You Can Grow Yourself

> **What You'll Learn:**
> Priced out of the produce market?
> Even if you don't have land, you can learn to grow fruits and vegetables in pots, tubs, and planters.

Here are a few quotations from a vegetable seed catalogue:

Asparagus: One ounce produces *600* roots. Cost per ounce: $5.95. (Have you priced a can of asparagus lately?)

Danvers Carrot: One ounce will plant a 300 foot row. Cost per ounce $2.85. (At this price you could feed them to your pig!)

Derby Day Cabbage: 7,000 seeds per ounce. Cost per ounce: $4.95. (Hmmm, let's see. 7,000 heads of cabbage at 45 cents each is...)

Red Sails Lettuce: ¼ ounce plants a hundred foot row. Cost per ounce: $3.65. (Made into salads they would fill a child's swimming pool.)

These quotes are intended to show you just how much you can add to your diet for little or no money. All you have to do is cultivate the soil and add the water and some exhilarating work; the bounty-bringing sun does all the rest.

Space

If you have room around your house for a half-acre garden (100 feet by 200 feet), it's enough to grow *all* the vegetables and small fruits that a *large* family can eat with *plenty left over* for canning, preserving, drying or selling to others.

Prices: (Mid-February 1995)

	February 1995	In-season
Tomatoes	$ .89 each	$ .49 each
Corn	$ .89 each	$ .29 each
Musk Melon	$1.49 per lb.	$ .49 per lb.
Strawberries	$1.99/basket	$ .99/basket
Raspberries	$1.99/basket	$ .99/basket
Asparagus	$3.99 per lb.	$1.99 per lb.

Seeds

It pays to buy the best seeds from a reputable seed firm. The cost involved is usually so small that it would be a false economy to use anything but the best. Here are a few of the many reputable seed firms in the U.S.

W. Atlee Burpee, 300 Park Avenue, Warminster, PA 18974
The Cook's Garden, PO Box 53528, Londonderry, VT 05148
Johnny's Seeds, 310 Foss Hill Road, Albion, ME 04910

Chapter Six
Food You Can Grow Yourself

Nichols Garden Nursery, 1190 North Pacific Highway, Albany, OR 97321
Park Seed Company, Cokesbury Road, Greenwood, SC 29647
Seeds West, PO Box 1739, El Prado, NM 87529
Vermont Bean Seed Company, Garden Lane, Fair Haven, VT 05743
Pinetree Garden Seeds, PO Box 300, New Gloucester, ME 04260

Soil and Seedlings

As anyone who has grown any plant knows, the constitution of the soil is of prime importance. It must contain the nutrients needed by the plant or else nothing happens. Rich soil produces lush plants. Here's an easy way to learn about your soil and to prepare your own mix for a seedling garden.

Procure a wooden lug box and place newspapers or cardboard over the holes to prevent the dirt from falling through but still permit drainage. Next, pour in one-third clean builder's sand, one-third manure or compost (the latter is simply the rotted remains of mixed vegetables) and one-third of the best top soil you can find in your neighborhood. Mix it well and dampen. Now use your finger or stick to "plow" a series of furrows about 3 inches apart. Sprinkle your seeds into the furrow and cover lightly. Sprinkle with water once more. Place your plants-to-be in a warm corner of your home and await results. In a week or less, the green sprouts (just like your salad sprouts) should poke through the soil. When this happens move the seedling flat to the light near a window and allow the sprouts to mature. Sprinkle lightly once a day.

Grow Your Own Seedlings:
1. Sprinkle seeds into furrows, cover lightly and water.
2. Nature takes care of germination.
3. A well-sprouted seedling bed ready for transplanting.
4. Cut individual plants apart just like a one-layer cake.
5. Transplant to prepared rows outdoors...
6. ...then protect with homemade shields.

Transplanting

When the weather permits (no more frosts) you can cut up the seedling box like a one-layer cake and move your seedlings outdoors. Remove as much of the original soil as possible and

Chapter Six
Food You Can Grow Yourself

place the tender new plants in a well-cultivated and well-manured or composted row. Leave plenty of room between plants; if you make a mistake, make it on the side of too much rather than too little room. This is especially true of plants like squash and pumpkin, which love to roam all over creation.

Your first-time-plants will look very vulnerable in their new, outdoor home because they are. You can protect them with homemade "tents" made from milk cartons, pieces of cardboard, or old shingles.

Watering your new transplants is a matter of judgment. If they begin to look withered, add water. If the soil is muddy, hold off for a few days. Soon you'll be able to judge by plant and soil appearance the amount of water to add. It's been established by experts that frequent light waterings are far better than periodic floodings. This allows the plant to breathe between inundations; air is as important to plant life as water, with a few exceptions.

No Room?

Don't have an outdoors? Live in a tight little city? Then just transplant your seedlings to pots, tubs, Number 10 tin cans, window boxes, planters and raised beds. The latter is simply a much larger seedling box placed on a fire escape, roof, or wherever you have room and there's sun. There are advantages to this method of horticulture; animals such as gophers and moles usually don't live in tubs and cans. Also, you'll be able to move your plants around to take advantage of the best sun and weather protection. Further, you'll be safe from hungry neighbors who might be thinking of a midnight raid on your carrot patch.

Another solution to space problems is communal growing of vegetables and small fruits. Is there an empty lot in your neighborhood? If so, why not gather a group together and find away to use the lot for a community garden? It's being done in many areas with enthusiasm. In these times of high costs and short supply, it makes good sense to try to alleviate both problems communally and reap the benefits of outdoor exercise at the same time.

Growing

Actually this is done by the plants themselves, not you, so there is not much to do except keep out bone-burying dogs, goats and pesky insects. A fence takes care of the first two and here are some suggestions on the latter:

1. *Pyrethrum:* dried, ground flower of oriental chrysanthemum. Also known as Dalmation powder.
2. *Rotenone:* Powder from roots (tropical) containing rotenone.
3. *Soap Spray:* 2 tablespoons soap flakes (not detergents) in 1 quart water.
4. *Nicotine Sulphate:* add to soap spray above. Bought as Black Leaf. Follow directions on label.
5. *Dusting Sulphur:* never use against house or fence as it discolors paint.
6. Same as Number 5 used with Pyrethrum.

Chapter Six
Food You Can Grow Yourself

7. *Water:* use as a fine strong spray, preferably in hand sprayer. Care not to flood.
8. *Mineral Oil Spray:* 3 parts oil/100 parts water.
9. *Wood Ash:* around base of plants to discourage cutworms.
10. *Epsom Salt Spray:* 2 ounces salt, 2 gallons water.
11. *Beer:* Stale or with molasses in saucer in garden.
12. *Ryanta:* root and woody stem of South American plant.
13. *Pepper:* hot peppers in water, or Cayenne pepper. Sprayed when plants are wet with dew.
14. *Bordeaux Mixture:* can be bought ready mixed.
15. *Borax and Icing Sugar:* mix together in equal parts, sprinkle on ground or rocks.
16. *Tomato Leaves Spray:* crush and soak in water, strain.
17. *Rhubarb Leaves:* boil 3 pounds leaves in 3 quarts of water. Strain, add to 1 ounce soap flakes dissolved in 1 quart water.
18. *Traps:* cutworms and millipedes come to surface at night. Use gloves and flashlight to catch them.
19. *Naphthalene:* dig into ground 2 ounces/10 square feet.
20. *Trap for Grasshoppers and Ants:* paraffin lined pill boxes or cans baited with sugar water, bacon rind, scraps. Drop filled traps in boiling water.
21. Encourage, buy, cultivate all bird life, ladybugs, praying mantises, spiders, lizards, salamanders, bats and toads for truly effective pest control.

Mulching

Weeds can be a problem but mulching your new plants with straw or grass cuttings can reduce the number of unwanted volunteers. Mulching means to cover the ground except where your desired plants are growing. An inch-size thickness is not too much, though a thinner protective layer would probably do the job. See the wonderful book on the subject of mulching by Ruth Stout listed below.

Harvesting

Nutritionally, all plants have a peak of goodness. Experimentation will tell you just when to pull the carrots and pick the corn. Certainly this is the fun part of growing your own foods, the delicious payoff that makes all your efforts worthwhile.

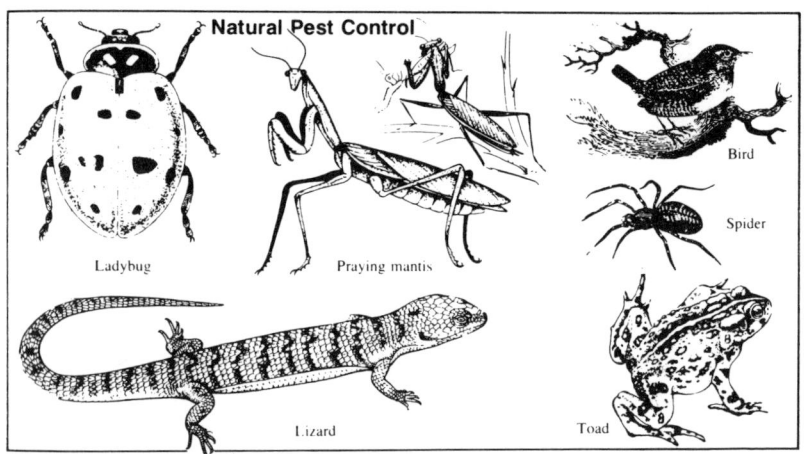

Natural Pest Control — Ladybug, Praying mantis, Bird, Spider, Lizard, Toad

Selected Bibliography for Gardening

Does the above sound simple, almost too easy? Well, that's because growing things for your own kitchen use really *is* simple. After all, think of the billions of tons of wild foods that plant themselves, fight off insects and marauders and produce a bountiful harvest without benefit of human intervention. That's why we recommend the casual approach to gardening — let nature do practically all the work since she knows best.

For further information, we suggest the following books from your local library or book store or direct from the publishers (some addresses are given).

The Sunset Garden Book, Lane Book Company, Menlo Park, CA 94025.

Chapter Six
Food You Can Grow Yourself

How to Have a Green Thumb Without an Aching Back, A New Method of Mulch Gardening, Ruth Stout, Exposition Press, 50 Jericho Turnpike, Jericho, NY 11753.

The Encyclopedia of Organic Gardening, J.I. Rodale, Rodale Press, Emmaus, PA 18049.

How to Grow Vegetables and Fruits by the Organic Method — Anyone Can Have A Green Thumb, A.D. Pardee, Hearthside Press, 381 Park Avenue South, NY 10016.

The Ex-Urbanites Complete and Illustrated Easy-Does-It-First-Time Farmers Guide, Bill Kaysing, Simon & Schuster.

Suburban and Farm Vegetable Gardens, U.S.D.A., Superintendent of Documents, U.S. Government Printing Office, Washington, D.C. 20402. This item is a 46-page booklet full of valuable information. Also, if you'll write the U.S.D.A. directly (Washington, D.C. 20250) and ask about problems related to your own area, they'll send you specific data. Another source is your state Department of Agriculture located in the capital of your state.

To sum up the reasons for growing your own:

- You'll save money for sure. Since a half-acre garden will produce more than enough for a large family, the value of the crop will be about equal to your present vegetable and small-fruit budget.
- Everyone in the family will enjoy growing their own favorite vegetables and small fruits.
- Your fruits and vegetables will be fresher and more healthful. In addition, since you won't use poison sprays, you'll be cutting down on the amount of insecticides you ingest.
- If you really do have a green thumb, you can sell the surplus output of your home garden and make a profit to buy things you don't grow.

And while you're growing your basics outside, why not cultivate the trimmings inside your house?

Grow Your Own Sprouts

Sprouts!! You can grow them fresh all year long, and right inside your kitchen at that. This is fresh food — indeed, it is growing food right up to the moment you consume it. Use sprouts raw in salads or sandwiches. Cooking them by steaming causes only a small loss in vitamin content.

Here's all you have to do. Soak a tablespoon of seeds overnight in a quart-size glass jar. Any kind of seeds can be used: alfalfa, beans (soy, mung, kidney, navy, or any other type), lentils, peas, sunflower seeds, and even wheat, oats, barley, and rye. Now place a piece of cheese cloth, nylon stocking, or other loosely woven fabric over the top of the jar and hold it in place with a rubber band or string. Next morning, pour out the water and place the jar in a warm, dark cupboard. Two or three times a day, take out the jar, pour in cool water to cover the seeds and pour it out again. This keeps the seeds moist but not wet, thus permitting them to sprout just as they would in the ground.

Alternatively, you can place your seeds on two layers of clean cloth, cover with two or more layers of clean cloth, soak the whole package, and allow to drain (placing them in a tray with drainage in the bottom is ideal). Then place in a dark spot and continue rinsing and draining as with the jar method. You can also buy all sorts of expensive equipment (heavy crocks, nozzles with fine spray attachments, etc.) but the results are the same as those you'll obtain with the no-cost jars or scrap cloth.

In three or four days, more or less, you'll find that the seeds have become beautiful crunchy sprouts. Those from mung beans will look just like the ones you have enjoyed in Chinese foods. They're ready for you to gobble up for the optimum in good nutrition. You can increase their chlorophyll content by placing them in direct sunlight for several hours. A window sill will do nicely. To use them, let your imagination run wild. Toss them in salads, mix them with any other vegetable combinations, add them to potato patties or rice dishes, or make the best sandwich imaginable with a layer of sprouts (preferably alfalfa), some sliced avocado, tomatoes, and mayonnaise.

Chapter Six
Food You Can Grow Yourself

When winter comes and fresh green vegetables are hard to come by, sprouted seeds are a great nutritional asset. They are loaded with Vitamin C and the B complex vitamins. One-half cup of soy sprouts, for instance, is equal in Vitamin C to six glasses of orange juice. In fact, sprouts contain all the known vitamins and are rich in potassium, phosphorous, and calcium. You get all of this food value by spending a few days waiting and a few pennies a pound. Let's say that you use mung beans to sprout; they sell for about $1.19 a pound. When sprouted they'll not only be far more nutritious than the original beans, they'll weigh from four to six times more than when they were dry. Thus, you'll be growing a fresh, multi-purpose vegetable in your own home for about 20 to 30 cents a pound and no waste!

The pioneers heading west drew on their sprouting experience to supplement their diet in another way. They let corn seeds become small plants and then ate the leaves. It was called corn salad and was often the only fresh food obtainable during the winter. I tried it and it works beautifully. Just buy some whole grain corn at your feed store, put it in a saucer and keep it just barely damp; the seeds will do the rest. If transplanted the sprouting corn makes a handsome indoor plant, too.

The Window Box Herb Garden

How about watching your own fresh herbs grow? Then bang together a simple structure that looks like this:

Fill it with rich soil and plant some herbs. Chives, parsley, and rosemary are easy to grow. Place the box just outside your kitchen window where the plants can enjoy the sun and you can enjoy their progress. If you live in a cold climate, set the box indoors and keep it within reach of the outdoor light. You'll have what amounts to a greenhouse in miniature.

Chives

Garlic

Parsley

Herbs can be grown from cuttings (mint for example) or seeds (dill) or bulbs (garlic). An excellent source of all herb materials and instructions is Nichols Nursery, 1190 N. Pacific Highway, Albany, OR 97321. See also *The Complete Book of Herbs,* K.N. Sanecki (Macmillan).

Here are some typical growing plans:

Chivescan be grown from seed or from existing bulb clumps. Divide the clumps and transplant to your window box or kitchen garden. They need lots of moisture and love shade. Pick off the flowers to keep the leaves, the edible part, growing. Cut with scissors and sprinkle over salads, chili, or cottage cheese for a brisk, oniony flavor.

Dill is best grown in your garden since it is a large plant. Sprinkle seeds along one edge. Thin to 18 inches apart and keep

Chapter Six
Food You Can Grow Yourself

well watered. When mature, the dried sprigs are added to pickles and such. The seeds alone make a tasty addition to many foods.

Basil is a favorite herb and grows easily and well almost anywhere. Sprinkle seeds, cover lightly and water frequently. You'll find that it grows prolifically. Great fresh or dried on and in such dishes as soybean loaf, spaghetti sauce, scrambled eggs and sliced tomatoes.

Sage is an herb that you don't have to grow if you live in the desert regions of the American southwest. You can pick enough leaves off this grey-green bush to last you a lifetime in just one stroll through the sand and cactus. If you're not a desert dweller, grow sage from seeds by sprinkling in a corner of your garden and watering sparingly. Add the leaves to turkey stuffing, or any dish where a strong and vigorous flavor is desired. Incidentally, the favorite Italian herb, oregano, is a variety of mountain sage.

Other herbs, such as tarragon, marjoram, caraway, mint, parsley, rosemary and thyme can be grown as easily as those mentioned above. So add to the flavor of what would otherwise be plain tasting foods with the addition of fresh and dried, home-grown herbs and spices.

Rosemary Sage

Watermint

Caraway

Chapter Seven

How To Preserve Your Perishables

What You'll Learn:
A number of ways to keep foods edible for long periods of time. These include drying, smoking, and dry and liquid storage.

The advantages of knowing some or all of the preserving methods is obvious. Let's say that someone presents you with a twenty-pound tuna or four five-pound barracudas. You eat what you can of the fresh fish, but what about the rest? Nothing tastes better than smoked fish, knowing how to smoke them will not only pay off financially; you'll reap a lot of pleasure from it as well.

The same holds true for a windfall of, say, fresh apricots. Perhaps you have made arrangements to pick them in some farmer's orchard for a few cents per pound. What you cannot eat fresh, you should try to preserve. A knowledge of drying, canning, freezing or other methods will make your winter more pleasant.

Drying

Homemade drying rack

The easiest way to preserve any food is to dry it. Dried fruits are delicious. Last year there were more pears on our tree than we could possibly eat, stew up or give away. Remembering how good the dried pears were that we once bought at a roadside fruit stand, we decided to try drying some of our own. We simply washed the pears and sliced them vertically, about four slices apiece, seeds, stem and all. Then we took off two of our window screens and hosed them off thoroughly. We laid one down and spread the sliced pears on it and then covered it with the other screen. The wooden frames touched each other and sealed out insects. To further ensure that the pears wouldn't be attacked, we placed the whole thing on top of the sloping roof of our house. Flies, we had learned, do not venture much higher than twenty feet from the ground. After two or three days, we turned all the pear slices over and put them up for another couple of days. When we brought them down, they were perfect — the moisture had been dried out yet they were still soft enough to eat. We then packed them into large jars, stirring them occasionally and finally sealing them tightly. Now, a year later, we are still enjoying the dried pears as an after-dinner treat. This is a perfect example of how to extend the bounties of summer through the less bountiful winter and spring periods. Incidentally, we did the same thing with a lug of apricots we bought for a dollar from a nearby farm; and our daughter had great success with a donated box of peaches.

Smoking

There's nothing quite like a chunk of well-smoked fish for flavor and economy (the latter applies especially if you have smoked it yourself). Many people believe that smoking fish (and other vittles) is a difficult process. Nothing could be further from the truth. All it takes to smoke fish is a source of smoke and some kind of container to retain the smoke.

Homemade smoking frame

One of the simplest arrangements consists of a small electric hot plate, available at any hardware store, and an enclosure made from wire and aluminum foil. If you already have the hot plate, you can build this entire rig for less than 50 cents and a few minutes of your time. First, get a length of heavy wire 25 feet long. The type used for coat hangers is easy to bend yet substantial enough for framework. (You can use coat hangers, if you wish. Just clip off the hook, straighten them out, and twist the ends together. Each one gives about 34 inches of wire.) Bend the wire into a simple, rectangular box about two feet long and one foot square (as shown in the drawing). Add some cross pieces from which to hang the food to be smoked; two or three will be plenty. Doubling the wire on these will prevent sagging under a heavy load. Cover the entire framework with aluminum foil and crimp the foil around the wire.

Next, obtain some hickory or other hard wood chips or sawdust and place them directly on the plugged-in hot plate. Cut up your fish or other food, pierce with plain wire and hang from the crosspieces inside your smoker. Carefully place the loaded smoker over the hot plate. Within a short time, the smoker will be full of warm, fragrant smoke.

You can regulate the amount of smoke and heat by turning the hot plate down or off periodically. A little practice will demonstrate how much smoke and heat to apply to a given quantity of fish or other food.

Ordinary fish, whole or in large chunks, will smoke through in less than one day of very low heat and minimal smoke. After all, fish is easily cooked. Meats will take longer, but then, we don't really recommend anyone eating U.S. meat since it is so loaded with chemicals as to be both worthless and dangerous to one's health.

This type of smoker can be used wherever electricity is available. If you are one of those fortunates who live far from modern civilization, you can build yourself an outdoor smoker as follows: Construct a wooden shelter to any convenient size, anywhere from a small shed to one perhaps six feet square and eight or ten feet tall. The wood can be logs or poles and the siding can be anything convenient. You can either place crosspieces inside from which to hang the fish, meat or hams, or build horizontal framed squares of ordinary one-inch mesh chicken wire on which to toss the food to be smoked.

Next dig a shallow pit or cover an area on the floor with cobble stones. What you want to achieve is a cool smoke; thus your fire should be small and made from green hardwoods such as oak, hickory, and birch. Alder, willow, and similar woods are fine, but stay away from the soft, sappy woods such as pine and fir. From here on, it's just common sense and some experience. Place your fish on the frames or hang them from the crosspieces. Build a *small,* smoky fire and then go about your business. You can expect

Chapter Seven
How To Preserve Your Perishables

the smoking process to do its flavorful work in twenty-four to forty-eight hours.

You can apply all kinds of fancy touches to the food before smoking. Try rubbing the pieces with spices, chili powder, honey, or garlic. If they are somewhat dry at the start, rub on some butter or a high-quality cooking oil.

By experimenting with this fascinating way to add good food at low cost to your table, you'll become a smoking expert in a short time.

Canning and Freezing

So much has been written by experts on these subjects that I refer you to their work. To find out how you can freeze and can surplus foods of all types, write for free U.S.D.A. booklets. Address your order to the United States Department of Agriculture, Washington, DC 20250 and ask for canning and freezing data.

These booklets consist of solid, no-nonsense information that can make you an expert in the field of home food preservation. If, as often happens, the food you preserve comes to you free, your only expense will be for the materials and time involved in preserving the food. Bradford Angier, who writes about living off the land (see his *How To Live in the Woods on $10 a Week),* describes how people who live in the wilder parts of the United States and Canada are able to acquire enough meat to last all year from just one organic moose or elk.

Dry and Liquid Storage Methods

In the October 1973 issue of *Organic Gardening and Farming,* there is a fine article on how to preserve foods in a very simple manner. Basically, it involves creating a root cellar where fruits and vegetables may be preserved in dry sand, hay, or other insulative materials. The major effort lies in building the various bins, and storage boxes to be fitted into an area with a dry, low-temperature environment. A layer of sand is spread on the bottom of each container. Then a layer of the food to be preserved, say carrots, is placed on the sand. Make sure that the individual vegetables do not touch each other. Cover the vegetables with another layer of sand and make another layer. Dry grains such as wheat and corn are placed in dry containers and kept cool and rodent-free. Incidentally, you can add a picturesque touch to your storage area/root cellar by hanging some ears of corn or bunches of dried herbs from the ceiling. Onions, squash, pumpkins, and other easy-to-store items are merely placed in the dry, cool storage area. Keeping ability depends on the original freshness of the food. All root crops can be preserved this way.

The Earnests, authors of the article, have originated a no-work method of liquid storage. For example, they place washed cucumbers in jars, add dry mustard, salt, and honey and fill the jars with vinegar. After shaking and sealing, the pickles make themselves in about two weeks. No heat, no cooking, no trouble.

Storage Methods

Other vegetables can be preserved in water-vinegar solutions or in dill brine made by diluting one cup of white vinegar with two cups of water and adding one or more sprigs of dill to suit your taste. Tomatoes, cabbage, cauliflower, and peppers keep well in this no-cooking, liquid preservative. As the Earnests say, "There's something very comforting about being surrounded by a winter's food — stepping around full bins in the cellar and ducking under swaying bunches in the attic, touching aromatic herbs whose fragrance at times fills the house. We all benefit. The whole family works together to bring in the harvest, which we enjoy at leisure during the cold months. I probably benefit most of all, spending less time bending over a hot stove cooking and preserving and more time outside watching the garden grow." That holds true no matter how you preserve your foods.

Preserving Eggs

You can buy sodium silicate, otherwise known as waterglass, at a drug supply house or hardware store. Place eggs in a jar and cover with this liquid. They'll keep for months simply because the sodium silicate shuts out all air. Or coat the eggs with wax, the heavier the coat the better. People packing stores for long boat voyages use this method and report good keeping qualities.

Chapter Eight

In Case You Have To

Use A Supermarket

What You'll Learn:
That most of the 8,000-odd items in a supermarket are not worth buying. What to avoid and why.

Did you ever admire the rows of beautiful rainbow-colored containers stacked neatly at the supermarket? Don't be naive enough to think the companies threw these colorful containers in for free. When you buy a fancy package, here's what you're paying for:

- The creative design
- Preliminary and final art work

- The very expensive color printing plates
- Printing press time and material
- The filling of the package by electrical machinery
- Further packaging in a shipping carton
- The labor to put the package out on the shelf
- The labor to check it out and put it in your take-home bag

That's a lot of bills for you to pay, and you should know that some packages cost as much as 20% of the item cost. When you shop, buy food; don't waste your money on inedible packages that clutter up your trash can and add to the waste pollution problem.

And while we're on the subject, when you shop for food, keep away from other sorts of products. Don't load your basket with cooking utensils, motor oil, clothing, and all the rest of the overpriced junk that the market would like you to buy. You can always buy these things for less in the proper store. Don't pay a hundred percent more for something just because it's convenient. As a matter of fact, when you need some item for the kitchen or the home, check your local flea market, rummage sale, Salvation Army, or Goodwill store first. You'd be amazed at how little you can pay for things at these outlets.

Skip Chewing Gum, Sugared or Sugarless

Of all the time-wasting, jaw-tiring, idiotic habits forced on people by advertising, the chewing of gum has to take one of the top trophies. Here's the problem: The sugared variety rots teeth. The non-sugared variety is expensive and creates a flow of digestive juices that trickles into the stomach for no useful purpose.

Soft Drinks

The average American drinks about twenty gallons of soft drink a year. The result is that soft-drink manufacturers get very rich and everyone else gets rotten teeth, among other things. You don't hear more about how destructive soft drinks are because the manufacturers spend millions of dollars on advertising to tell you

Chapter Eight
In Case You Have To Use A Supermarket

how wonderful their products are. The people who control the media don't dare bite the hand that feeds them, and no one else can outspend the big spenders in opposition advertising. Sugar in any form is poison, and every twelve-ounce bottle of soft drink has about six teaspoons of sugar in it. Just ask an honest doctor or dentist to tell you the truth about soft drinks. For example, Dr. D.A. Collins writes in *Your Teeth, A Handbook of Dental Care for the Whole Family*, "Families that allow concentrated refined sugars, particularly in the form of cookies, cakes, candies and sweetened beverages, make the child dependent on sweets. With the development of his sweet tooth will come a high incidence of cavities. The results will be pain, loss of teeth, high dental bills and deformed mouths."

If that doesn't convince you, take a look at some more dramatic evidence.

> At the Naval Medical Research Institute we put human teeth in cola beverage and found that they softened and started to dissolve within a short period. They became soft within two days.
> In the intervening years 1943-1950 we have made numerous studies of the effect of these cola beverages upon the teeth of rats, dogs and monkeys. One of our technicians became so expert in judging the conditions of the surface of the molar teeth of rats that she could tell those that had had one drink of cola beverage amounting to 2½ teaspoons or 10 milliliters. We have published data indicating that the molar teeth of rats are dissolved down to the gum line, if the rats are well fed but given nothing to drink except cola beverage for a period of six months. (*Journal Nutrition*, 1949. Vol. 39. p. 313.)
>
> Data has been published indicating that the cola beverages contain substantial amounts of caffeine. These cola beverages deserve careful consideration not only in relation to our national problem of poor teeth but in relation to our numerous cases of gastric ulcers, and welfare of our children.
> The acidity of cola beverages, which the biochemist expresses as pH, is 2.6 or about the same as vinegar. The sugar

content masks the acidity and children little realize they are drinking this strange mixture of phosphoric acid, sugar, caffeine, coloring and flavoring matter. (*The Prevention Method for Better Health,* J. I. Rodale and staff.)

Although a healthy liver is vital to well-being and is perhaps the main defense against cancer, the incidence of liver damage in the United States, including often fatal cirrhosis, is said to be increasing rapidly even among children. This problem once confined to chronic alcoholics is now common among social drinkers, overweight individuals, people harmed by drugs or chemicals, and those whose diets are inadequate.

Some physicians consider that the appalling consumption of soft drinks — 60 million bottles daily of one brand alone — is a major cause. (*Let's Get Well,* Adelle Davis; Harcourt Brace Jovanovich, Inc.)

It's just not worth it to give in to your children when they beg for the junk Madison Avenue is hawking.

Instead of buying soft drinks, make your own from healthful ingredients. Serve fresh orange juice, apple juice, and milk drinks with non-sugar flavorings. Or try a punch with lots of ice, lemon juice, grapefruit or pineapple juice.

Candy, Cakes, and Cookies

Sugar is a non-food and has no place on your dinner table, so you can scratch these items permanently. Not only will you save shopping money, but you'll save money on doctor and dentist bills at the same time. In addition, you'll enjoy better health, more energy, and longer life. Here are some alternatives to sugar-filled junk foods:

- honey (but go easy)
- fresh fruits
- sesame seeds
- peanut butter
- cashew butter

- nuts of all kinds
- coconut
- citron
- prunes
- dates
- carob confections
- melons

Snacks

One of the easiest ways to exceed your budget while strolling down the aisles of a market is to pick up those tempting packages of snack goods. Just imagining the taste of potato chips, the satisfying crunch of corn chips, or the filling, salty chompiness of pretzels is enough to make some people reach for one or more of these snack foods automatically. On top of that, children who have been introduced to these fun-to-eat tidbits keep clamoring for more — aided and abetted, of course, by an endless stream of commercials on TV.

There are several good reasons for avoiding this pitfall. One has to do with the high cost of the snack items relative to the amount of food actually in the package. Regarding potato chips, for instance, divide the weight of the contents into the price of the package, and you discover that you are being charged over 2 dollars per pound for food that costs less than 20 cents per pound in the vegetable department. The second and equally important reasons for avoiding snack foods is that most of them are fried in deep fat. The combination of starch with hot fat is one of the most indigestible and harmful mixtures you can eat, as almost any doctor will tell you. Do your family the favor of resisting these foods. You'll find ideas for healthful substitutes throughout this book.

Coffee and Tea

With beverage prices rising out of sight along with everything else, and caffeine under study for its effects on the human heart, it's time to start thinking in terms of healthy do-it-yourself beverages. Almost any grain such as wheat, barley, or rye can be coarsely ground, roasted in the oven and used to make a palatable boiled or percolated beverage. These substitutes were commonly employed in wartime by various nations whose supply of coffee was limited.

Tea is even easier. For example, there's wild mint growing just about everywhere in the United States. Gather some, dry it, and use the leaves just as you would ordinary tea leaves. You may want to try some of the more exotic teas such as comfrey, sassafras, alfalfa, and birch. All are tasty; most are better for you than the imported leaf.

While we're on the subject of drink, it's important that you make certain that your drinking water is pure. If it isn't, buy distilled drinking water, distill tap water yourself (there are small distillers now on sale), or obtain your water from a spring known to be pure. There's no point in eating healthy foods if the water you drink isn't first rate.

Alcoholic Beverages

One of the fastest ways to run your food bill up is to buy a lot of alcoholic beverages. While I'm not on the stump on behalf of the teetotalers of the world, I *am* on the stump to keep your food bills down.

Alcoholic beverages — beer, wine, whiskey, vodka, brandy, rum, etc. — are not foods by any stretch of the imagination. Therefore, if you are really concerned about your ever-mounting food bills, buy a hundred pounds of whole wheat instead of a bottle of medium-priced bourbon. The wheat will last you much longer, give you much greater returns health-wise, and will come in a lot handier a lot more often. And you can't get a hangover from home-baked bread.

But if you just can't do without a little nip now and then, a couple of recipes for homemade wine follow. These are old farmstyle methods that work as well today as they did when they were recorded in the mid-1800s.

Chapter Eight
In Case You Have To Use A Supermarket

A legal point first: You can make up to 200 gallons of wine a year for home use if you obtain a license from the Alcohol Tax Unit of the Internal Revenue Service. If you want to go into distilled liquors, then you've got to talk at length with these same people.

Blackberry Wine

Gather the berries when ripe on a dry day, measure and bruise them. To every gallon of berries add 1 quart of boiling water. Let the mixture stand 24 hours, stirring occasionally. Strain off the liquor into a cask, and to every gallon add one pound of honey. Cork tight and let it stand until October and you will have wine for use without any further steaming or boiling.

Grape Wine

Heat the grapes slightly in a large kettle with very little water and then crush through a strainer until you have one quart of juice. To this add 3 quarts of water and 2½ pounds of honey. Keep in an open barrel for 19 days, covering with muslin to protect from insects. Then put in a closed cask, fasten and bung, and set aside until spring. Then rack off and bottle.

These recipes are simple to follow if you have the correct ingredients and equipment. To make your finished product especially appealing, make up some labels on parchment paper.

They can be printed from a wood block or simply written by hand with an old goosequill.

Chain Restaurants

Chain restaurants are cousins to supermarkets. If you ever sit in on a board meeting for a large restaurant chain, you won't believe your ears. The customer has absolutely no status at all. He only exists as a body to fill up a seat, a stomach to be filled with the cheapest food dispensed at the highest prices. Most of the places seek to delude you into thinking you've been well fed at the end of a meal. They cater, of course, to the person who thinks that a fried piece of meat on a plastic sponge bun is a meal in itself. Almost everything served in a typical chain is fried, and the soup is a concoction of chemicals warmed in plain tap water. Ugh, I could go on for pages. But your own sense of taste will convince you. Do yourself a favor. Carry something good to eat wherever you go and leave the chain restaurants to languish in their fried-fat fumes.

Chapter Nine

What You Should Know

About Sugar

What You'll Learn:

That sugar is a slow (sometimes not so slow) poison.

Author's note: We are grateful to Mick and Lini of the LA *Free Press* for this definitive and forceful review of a product that comprises as much as half of some American diets.

This week, in answer to many requests we've had from our readers, we'd like to talk about sugar and what its effects are on the human body. Of all the foods we eat, sugar is one of the most harmful and there are myriad reasons for avoiding it.

- The sugar we usually eat is not a whole food but rather the extract of a tropical plant. When we eat sugar our body's automatic response is to swallow it without chewing it.
- Sugar is extremely alkaline. When we swallow it the stomach is paralyzed for one to three minutes by the shock it produces on our system. In reaction to this strong alkaline substance, the stomach secretes a tremendous amount of acid in an attempt to neutralize it.
- When the sugar leaves the stomach it takes this excess acid with it and enters the duodenum, still in an undigested form. Because of this excess acid, the duodenum lets it pass through again without neutralizing it and consequently it goes on to pollute the rest of the body.
- In order to digest sugar the intestines have to draw on the mineral reserve in the body and this produces tooth decay, falling hair and weak bone structure. (It might be interesting for you to know that the condition of the teeth is a good indication of the condition of the entire skeleton.) In addition, since a great deal of oxygen is consumed during this process, there is a shortage of oxygen in the brain and consequently the mental capacity is reduced.
- When the sugar reaches the blood stream even more problems arise. Our pancreas is designed to deal only with natural sugars. When it encounters a substance as powerful as refined sugar one of two things can happen. Since it is the function of the pancreas to neutralize sugar, there is a panic reaction and a great deal of insulin is secreted. If the pancreas is weak and this condition continues, diabetes may develop. In most cases, however, the pancreas is strong enough to remain operative and it secretes *too much* insulin. This neutralizes most of the sugar in the blood. The result is hypoglycemia — low blood sugar, a condition which nine out of ten Americans suffer from to some degree.
- Hypoglycemia manifests itself in countless ways. Some of the symptoms are tiredness, irritability, sudden fits of anger, irrationality, poor memory and hostility. If you have ever suddenly found yourself exhausted for no apparent reason and desiring sweets then there is a good chance that you are suffering from low blood sugar.
- The problem becomes more complicated because when you have hypoglycemia you are drawn to even more sugar. If you eat more sugar you will feel better for a while, but soon you will start to feel

Chapter Nine
What You Should Know About Sugar

tired and listless again. The only way of remedying this is by eating more sugar. In this manner, sugar produces an addiction that is just as real and powerful as that of any drug.

- When hypoglycemia develops our mentality suffers greatly. We become prone to fear, anxiety, worry, hatred, sudden fits of violence. It becomes easy for us to lie since our judgment is so clouded that it is difficult for us to see that in many cases it would be easier for us to tell the truth.
- Mothers who indulge their children's sweet tooth with sugar are often repaid with temper tantrums and unruly behavior. The child who screams and cries constantly is almost invariably a lover of sweets. If the wise parent removes all sweets from the child's diet there will be an almost miraculous improvement in the child's behavior within a very short time.
- Much of the food available in the so-called health food stores contains brown sugar or yellowed sugar. There is a general superstition among health-minded people that these sugars are in some way superior to refined white sugar. In reality, however, brown sugar is simply refined sugar with molasses added again to give it color. Sugar is sugar, regardless of what it is called or what color it is, and should be avoided at all times.
- Since sugar is so powerfully alkaline, it will burn the tongue of a baby. Only after repeated use do our tastes become so jaded that we enjoy it. If you refrain from eating sugar for several months and then try eating it, you too will find the taste unpleasant and the reaction it produces both immediate and powerful. If you cease using sugar your taste will gradually return to natural proportions, and if you chew your food very thoroughly you will be surprised at the sweetness you will discover in such simple foods as carrots, squash, onions, and grains.
- Many of you may be asking the question "What about honey or molasses?" These are merely another form of sugar and should also be avoided for the same reasons. Although honey is a natural substance, it has almost the same effect upon the human body as sugar. Molasses is nothing more than the pulp that remains after sugar has been refined. Although this may be disheartening you owe it to yourself to let your body have a chance to develop its natural tastes again. Honey causes your taste to become jaded in the same manner as sugar does. If you stop eating it for a while, you will not

only be giving your body a much needed rest, but you will have the opportunity to taste the real SWEETNESS of foods that you would have missed otherwise. If, after not eating honey for some time, you find yourself drawn to it again, by all means have some. The taste will be less stimulating than you imagined it would be and you will find that you are listless and grouchy the following day.

- The only way to cure hypoglycemia is to stop eating sugar and other sweets. Although you may have a reaction it will soon pass and your energy will return. Foods that generally assist the body in overcoming hypoglycemia are brown rice, aduki beans and squash.

Now, that's a powerful indictment of a product that is consumed in large quantities in America. The average person is believed to consume about a third of a pound of sugar per day. What do others say about this non-food item (non-food in the sense that it contributes nothing but calories)?

Natural Sugar
Honey bee
Banana (Plantain)
Strawberry
Apple

"Sugar is a nutritionally bankrupt substance...," says Frances Dahl, Nutritionist with the Marin County Department of Health. And Dr. John Yudkin, a University of London nutritionist and

Chapter Nine
What You Should Know About Sugar

author of *Sweet and Dangerous,* suggests that sugar is involved in coronary artery disease and adds that evidence against sugar is even more conclusive than it is against cholesterol.

Harvard professor of nutrition, Dr. Jean Mayer reports that 100 pounds of sugar is equal to 57 pounds of body fat (just about what many people have in excess weight).

One of the major problems with sugar is that it is present in almost all prepared foods. And even though the cost of sugar is rising it is still found in such seemingly innocent foods as bouillon cubes and non-dairy creamer. Further, sugar is the major ingredient in many items such as cola drinks, cake and donuts.

One of the great pioneers in nutritional research, J.I. Rodale, contributed an immense store of basic information concerning sugar and its effect on the human body. In one of his classic volumes, *The Complete Book of Food and Nutrition,* the many condemning references to sugar ought to convince any intelligent reader to exclude this non-food from his or her diet. Here is an example (but we recommend that you read it for yourself in the nearest library or bookstore):

> Concentrated pure sugar is a drug, unrelated to anything that occurs naturally. It throws off the calcium-phosphorus balance and disrupts this important phase of your body machinery. Because it has been robbed of its B vitamins, it latches on to these wherever it finds them — namely in your digestive tract. Thus, the person who eats sugar is bound to be short on B vitamins. Result? Nervousness, skin troubles, digestive problems and a host of other disorders which lead to much more serious trouble later on.

Rodale points out that sugar substitutes — molasses, maple syrup, and honey — are also fraught with hazards and he advises readers not to consume too much of them.

Rodale's book goes on to quote a speech given by M.H. Walsh, instructor in clinical nutrition at the University of California. In it, Walsh replies to the contention that sugar is a food by saying that if it were, it would be fed to animals by hog, beef, and poultry producers. The fact that sugar is not fed to these animals is solid proof that sugar is not really a food but rather a profit-making condiment/flavoring.

In reviewing Rodale's material further we find that sugar is responsible for dental caries (cavities), low blood sugar (eating sugar brings up the level momentarily but it plunges down as natural insulin is circulated), asthmas, alcoholism, neuroses, fatigue, rheumatic fever, ulcers, depression and on through a medical chamber of horrors.

From the author's own experience comes this true tale. A nephew had a kneecap removed surgically because it no longer functioned as a kneecap. In tracing back the problem it was discovered that the young boy had been drinking a six-pack of a common cola each and every day for years. Apparently, the phosphoric acid in the cola leached out all the calcium in the boy's system including that behind the kneecap. He had continued to drink the sugar-loaded soft drink, he would have ended up with no skeleton.

Conclusion

There's lots of evidence around that sugar is the worst nutritional enemy of many people. So why not try this test? Eliminate all or nearly all sugar from your diet for six weeks or so. See if you don't feel peppier, less tired at the end of the day, have better digestion and, not incidentally, save lots of money. With sugar at an all time high price, it's an expensive means to bad health. By no sugar we mean no bakery products, candy, ice cream, soft drinks, chewing gum, canned fruit, and so forth. Satisfy your conditioned sugar hunger with fresh fruit, raisins, dates, and such.

Sugarbeet

Part 2

How To Cook

For 99¢ A Meal

Chapter Ten

The Golden Rule:

Eat Less, Waste Nothing

> **What You'll Learn:**
>
> How to develop an attitude about how much food you really need, and how to use what you don't eat.

The first man to warn against overeating lived in medieval Europe. Luigi Cornaro, a 16th century Venetian, came from a wealthy family and wasted his early years in such riotous living, drunkenness and gluttony that by the time he was forty, degenerative disease threatened to kill him. Given no hope by his physicians, Cornaro retired to a small country estate and took stock of himself. He was an intelligent man; well-educated for his times, and capable of solid reasoning. He came to the conclusion that the human body was designed to function most efficiently and well on the minimum amount of food it takes to maintain normal weight and strength. Overeating was not simply a waste of food but a definite strain and burden on the body organs. He decided to experiment on himself and found that an intake of about fourteen ounces of solid food daily, with a pint of wine, best satisfied his particular needs. He ate only the plainest and simplest foods: coarse whole grain bread, a little meat — and usually fowl — and a green salad. Calorie values were unknown five hundred years ago, so Cornaro concerned himself only with quantity.

He found that in his own case the balance between enough and too much was so delicate, due to his damaged organs, that the addition of only two ounces more than he required would produce a severe digestive disturbance. This was perhaps fortunate, for it strengthened his already formidable resolve, and he was able to stick to his diet so faithfully that he regained his health. He became a noted architect and one of the leading citizens of the powerful Venetian republic, fathered a large family, and lived comfortably to the ripe old age of 102.

Cornaro wrote of his experiences and advised others to follow his example, but he prescribed no diets, and suggested that each person should experiment with the needs of his own body to discover the kinds of food and the minimum amount of food necessary to maintain health, weight and vigor. He recognized that this would vary with the individual and the kind of exercise and work performed. But, although Cornaro's work has been widely read, translated into many languages, and published many times over, people rarely show the resolution and will-power to follow his advice. One notable exception was John D. Rockefeller, Sr., who recovered his health and lived to the age of 96 through careful attention to a minimum diet. In his case, as in Cornaro's, it must be pointed out that severe digestive troubles made Rockefeller's attention to diet imperative. For most of us, food and the pleasures of eating are so important that we can seldom summon the will-power to practice such Spartan restraint. But the closer we come to

Chapter Ten
The Golden Rule: Eat Less, Waste Nothing

ingesting minimal individual requirements, the greater will be our reward in improved health and comfortable long life.

If you have ever gone into your kitchen looking for something to eat and found nothing appealing, you probably felt disappointed. But this momentary disappointment is a small price to pay for a slender and healthy body. And if you do manage to keep your kitchen completely free of snacks and excess food items except for fresh fruit, vegetables, seeds and nuts, the temptation to constantly nibble on something will slowly go away.

I recall a friend who was extremely fond of little cans of deviled ham. He would purchase them in quantity and eat them whenever he felt a bit hungry, frustrated, or simply bored. His weight began creeping up because with these prepared meats he usually had crackers and a glass of milk. The 300 or 400 calories that he added to his daily diet this way was all that was required to produce a steady and inexorable weight gain. One day, in discussing this with him casually, I suggested that the simplest way to break his habit was just not to buy the little cans of ham in the first place. He took the advice and not only did he save money, his weight returned to normal. A common sense approach? You bet it is, but one that unfortunately many millions of Americans do not practice.

Another friend of ours, who had moved away several years ago, kept lamenting in her letters about the way she was gaining weight. Recently we spent a week visiting in her home and found out why. Each evening before dinner it was her custom to serve drinks. This in itself was not the culprit, since she never had more than one martini. But the cocktail hour was an excuse for her to drag out all manner of tasty little appetizers and snacks — cheeses, olives, smoked oysters, sardines, dips, chips and crackers. While we sat there chatting, our friend continually helped herself to these high caloric appetizers. Since she ate only a modest dinner after this (small wonder!), she couldn't understand why those pounds kept adding up. After I added up the calories contained in her nibbling, she saw the light. Not only was she consuming *more* calories during the cocktail hour than she did for dinner, but the money it took to buy these extravagant little goodies often surpassed the outlay for the entire dinner.

You'll find these suggestions repeated throughout this book, but here again are the basic rules for cutting down on food intake:

- Buy only natural foods in their natural state.
- Buy no convenience or snack foods whatsoever.
- Prepare a shopping list if you do have to shop at a conventional market. This is most important, since the Madison Avenue boys sit up nights developing ways to coax you into buying snack foods on impulse. So take your shopping list, wear a pair of blinders, and march though the traps with the resolute purpose of buying only the items on your list, the foods you need to stay healthy and retain your normal weight.
- Go easy on even the good stuff. Follow the example of our old friend, Luigi, the Slender Italian Renaissance Man.
- Remember that human beings need a good balance of five elements: carbohydrates**Error! Bookmark not defined.**, fats, protein, vitamins, and minerals. A well-balanced meal will provide these necessities in their proper proportions. To tip the balance with in-between-meal snacks is unnecessary and wasteful.

Waste Nothing

Consider this: If you lose twenty percent of the food value of the things you buy in just plain physical waste, another twenty percent due to improper cooking (heating destroys vitamins), and still another twenty percent in failure to digest properly, it's possible that more than half of what you buy goes down the assorted drains. Corrective measures are in order: (1) Don't waste a speck; (2) cook foods as little as possible to preserve their nutritional values; and (3) eat correctly and exercise to make sure your body is able to extract the full nutritional value from the foods you eat.

Chapter Ten
The Golden Rule: Eat Less, Waste Nothing

Cook adequate servings, just enough for one meal, particularly for foods that are unpalatable when reheated. But if you do have leftovers, use them as shown in the chart below.

The French have a centuries-old method for using everything up. It's call the "pot au feu," and is a kettle of soup that simmers on the back of most country people's stoves all the time. This ever-new dish contains bits of everything that might have gone to waste. Naturally, it changes its character and flavor as days go by and that's good. Try this in your quest for good eating for less money.

How to Use Your Leftovers

Egg yolks: baked custard, homemade noodles, mock hollandaise sauce, scrambled eggs

Egg whites: meringue, soufflés

Hard cooked egg or yolk: casseroles, egg sauce, garnish, salads, sandwiches, thousand island dressing

Sour Cream: salad dressing, sauce for vegetables

Buttermilk: quick breads

Cooked chicken and fish: casseroles, creamed foods, curries, patties, potpies, salads, sandwiches

Cooked snap beans, lima beans, corn, peas, carrots: casseroles, creamed dishes, salads, sauces, scalloped vegetables, soups, stews, vegetables in cheese sauce

Cooked leafy vegetables, chopped: creamed or scalloped vegetables, omelets, soufflés, soups

Vegetable cooking liquid: gravies, sauces, soups, stews

Cooked rice, noodles, macaroni, spaghetti: baked macaroni and cheese, casseroles, macaroni salad, Spanish rice

Cooked potatoes: fried or creamed potatoes, potatoes in cheese sauce, salads, soups, stews or chowders

Cooked or canned fruits: fruit cups, fruit sauces, gelatin desserts, prune cake, quick breads, salads, shortcake, yeast breads

Fruit cooking liquids or fruit syrups: fruit cups, fruit sauces, fruit drinks, gelatin mixtures, tapioca puddings

Cooked wheat, oat or corn cereals: fried cereal, soufflés, puddings

Bread: bread pudding, croutons, dry crumbs for breading poultry or fish, fondues, French toast, salmon loaf, sardine puff, stuffings.

Chapter Eleven

Sample 99¢ Menus

When the original version of this book, *Eat Well On A Dollar A Day*, was written in the early and mid-seventies, it was easily possible to prepare three nutritious meals for just one dollar. Today, despite many food price increases, it is STILL possible but requires some effort and a shift to food items which are still very inexpensive such as whole grain, home-prepared items such as yogurt and food you grow yourself. Although there may be less overall variety there is compensation in having a diet that is close to the optimum in terms of being natural, unprocessed and economical.

Here is proof that the original title of the book maintains its validity.

A Typical Well-Balanced Menu
For Two!

Breakfast: two giant bowls of hot, organic oatmeal adorned with sprouts, honey and milk.

Lunch: Wild and garden salad with herb, olive oil and vinegar dressing. Toasted homemade sourdough cheese bread. Fresh fruit.

Dinner: Tofu burgers on buns with all the usual hamburger trimmings. Cinnamon-rice pudding.

Cost Analysis, Well-Balanced Menu

Breakfast	Cost in cents	Wt. oz.
hot oatmeal	.14	20
honey	.08	2
crisped sprouts	.04	2
skim milk	.20	8
Total	.46	32

Lunch		
wild and garden greens	.00	6
dressing	.20	2
homemade sourdough	.15	12
Parmesan	.20	1
Fruit	.20	10
Total	.75	31

Dinner		
Tofu burger	.60	16
rice pudding	.19	16
Total	.79	32

Total for two or $1/day	$2.00	3 lb./person

Oatmeal and Sprouts with Honey and Milk

Simmer oatmeal, add other items to individual taste. Crisp sprouts are homegrown sprouts (rye, alfalfa, or wheat) which have been dried.

Wild and Garden Salad

Gather as available, wash and tear into bite-size pieces. Mix dried wild herbs (rosemary, thyme, sage) with olive oil and vinegar, add to salad and toss.

Chapter Eleven
Sample 99¢ Menus

Toast bread and sprinkle with Parmesan. Seasonal fruit for dessert.

Tofu Burger

Mix $3/4$ cup of soy flour with sufficient cold water to make a paste. Beat until airy. Add 2 cups boiling water and cook for 5 minutes. Add 6 tsp. of lemon juice and stir. Curds will form just as though you were making cheese. Ladle the curds into a cloth-lined strainer and press out moisture with a weighted lid. Tofu will become firm as you chill it with cold water. Combine slices with onions, garlic, grated carrot and chopped green peppers. Form into patties and sauté in unhydrogenated soy oil until light and crisp. Add buns or sourdough slices with the usual hamburger treats... mustard, mayo, and ketchup.

Rice Pudding

Simmer $1/4$ cup of brown rice in 1 cup water until tender. Add a bit of cinnamon and the grated rind of half an orange. Enjoy.

Commentary on sample menus which follow...

Recipes and menus are virtually the same as in the first edition. Changes that appear reflect a major reorientation... dropping meat and for good reasons.

Prices have been updated. However, and surprisingly, many basic items are still modestly priced.

The most important aspect of this: meals are simple, nutritious and easy to prepare. Even at two or three dollars a day per person, they would be healthful bargains. But if you grow some of your own food, gather wild items and live frugally, you'll be able to stay quite close to the 99¢-a-day concept.

Eat Well For 99¢ A Meal

Another Typical Well-Balanced Menu

Breakfast: Honey-Almond Brown Rice Delight, Milk, Sliced Fresh Oranges

Lunch: Savory Onion Sandwich, Homebaked Bread, Butter, Dates

Dinner: Enchiladas Baja, Sprout, cabbage and green pepper salad, Watermelon wedges

Honey-Almond Brown Rice Delight

4 tablespoons brown rice
1 tablespoon shelled almonds

1 tablespoon honey
2 cups skim milk (reconstituted)

Simmer rice until tender. Add chopped almonds and honey. Serve with milk, warmed if desired.

Savory Onion Sandwich

Sauté a large chopped onion in some olive oil. Toast two whole wheat hamburger buns at the same time. Add your favorite hamburger trimmings and warm onions for a treat that tastes great and avoids the cost and health risks of meat.

Enchiladas Baja

1 tablespoon oil
$1/2$ cup soy analog
$1/2$ cup onion, chopped
1 clove garlic, minced
4 tortillas
4 olives

$1/2$ cup tomato sauce
1 tablespoon chili powder
4 tablespoons grated cheese
salt, pepper

Chapter Eleven
Sample 99¢ Menus

Sauté chopped onion in oil. Presoak soy analog to hydrate. When softened, add to onions and garlic and simmer 5 minutes. In separate pan, simmer tomato sauce with chili powder and seasonings for 5 minutes. Heat additional oil in frying pan and dip tortillas in for a few seconds on each side. Then dip in tomato sauce and lay on dish. Fill with one-fourth of soy mixture, add 1 tablespoon grated cheese and roll up. Pour remaining sauce on top and garnish with olives. Bake at 350° for 20 minutes.

Sprout, Cabbage and Green Pepper Salad

4 tablespoons mung bean sprouts   2 tablespoons oil
4 tablespoons finely shredded cabbage   1 tablespoon vinegar
1 tablespoon minced green pepper   salt, pepper

Toss mixed greens with oil, vinegar and seasonings.

Homebaked Sourdough Bread or Buns

4 cups freshly ground whole wheat flour
pinch of salt
water to mix

Mix 4 tablespoons flour with a little warm water. Let stand in saucer at room temperature for five days, stirring each day. When fermented, add to remaining flour in bowl and add sufficient water to make a stiff batter. Turn out on floured board and knead thoroughly. Then let the dough rise in a warm place until double in size. Punch down, knead again and let rise a second time. Turn into greased baking pan, let rise and bake at 350° for one hour.

Most nutritionists would deem this a well-balanced diet, since the emphasis is on fresh fruits, vegetables and grains.

The portions derived from these recipes are more than adequate. The total weight of all three meals is three and a half pounds per person. It is obvious that there will be extra food for a child or guest, or something left over the next day.

Cost Analysis, Well Balanced Menu

	Cost in cents	Cooked Weight (ounces)
Breakfast:		
Brown rice	.05	6
Almonds	.20	1
Honey	.08	1
Skim Milk	.35	16
Two Whole Oranges	.32	12
Total	1.00	36
Lunch:		
Onion	.20	16
Buns (2)	.20	6
Trimmings	.20	12
Dates (2)	.08	1
Total	.68	35
Dinner:		
Soy analog	.04	4
Tortillas	.15	4
Onion	.05	4
Tomato sauce	.10	4
Chili powder	.04	--
Garlic clove	.02	--
Olives	.12	1
Cheese	.28	2
Sprouts	.05	3
Cabbage	.10	4
Green pepper	.10	1
Oil & Vinegar	.13	3
Watermelon wedges	.10	8
Total	1.28	38
Grand Totals	2.96	109

Chapter Eleven
Sample 99¢ Menus

Suggested Menu for Two Featuring a Big Breakfast

Breakfast: Western pancakes, Honey/Butter/Walnuts Syrup, Roasted grain coffee or mint tea

Lunch: Potatoes with Cheese Sauce, Sliced cucumbers, splash of wild apple vinegar, Fresh pears

Dinner: Tossed Salad with Potato Mayonnaise, Banana Spice Bars, Alfalfa Tea

Western Pancakes

To ½ pound freshly ground whole wheat flour, add two large eggs, ¼ cup of spray process dry milk, ¼ cup fresh ground corn meal, ¼ cup safflower or soy oil, pinch salt and water to mix into a cream-like batter. Pour on hot oiled griddle to make 3- to 4-inch diameter cakes. Turn when bubbles form. Serve piping hot with syrup made from melted butter, honey and chopped walnuts. Terrific!

Wild Apple Vinegar

Gather wild apples, core and crush. Strain juice into bottles and allow to ferment naturally. Presto! Free, pure, organic vinegar for your salads.

Tossed Salad

To domestic greens such as lettuce and romaine, add poke, dandelion and other wild salad materials that cost no more than the time to gather them.

Potato Mayonnaise

½ cup baked mashed potato
1 teaspoon dry mustard
¾ cup cold pressed oil

2 tablespoons wild apple vinegar
dash salt if desired

Add mustard, salt and 1 tablespoon vinegar to mashed potato and rub through fine sieve. Beat briskly while adding remaining vinegar and oil.

Alfalfa Tea

Another freebie. Gather wild alfalfa, dry and crumble. Use like regular tea leaves. Delicious and healthful. A bit of mint will perk it up if you wish.

This menu begins with a substantial breakfast, continues with a good solid lunch and then tapers off with a light dinner. Many people sleep better if they go easy on the chow late at night. Try it yourself and see what happens.

Cost Analysis, Big Breakfast

	Cost in cents	Cooked Weight (ounces)
Breakfast:		
Wheat flour	.12	8
Eggs (2)	.20	4
Milk	.08	4
Corn meal	.03	2
Oil	.11	2
Butter	.12	1
Honey	.15	2
Walnuts	.15	1
Grain Coffee	.02	8
Total	.98	32

Chapter Eleven
Sample 99¢ Menus

Lunch:			
Potato/Cheese		.56	16
Cucumbers		.15	46
Wild Vinegar		--	1
Pears		.55	12
	Total	*1.26*	*75*
Dinner:			
Lettuce		.28	6
Wild Salad		--	3
Mayonnaise		.36	4
Alfalfa Tea		--	16
	Total	.64	29
Grand Totals		2.88	94

Vegetarian Menu One

Breakfast: Homemade yogurt with sunflower seeds, raisins, and walnuts, Whole wheat toast with butter and honey, Anise tea

Lunch: Minestrone, Crackers and cheese, Fruit of the season

Dinner: Eggplant Parmesan, Refried Beans, Dates, Homemade roasted-grain coffee

Homemade Yogurt

(Recipe given in Chapter Five). Add seeds and other items to taste.

Anise Tea

Seeds of anise plant may be gathered wild. Steep like tea. Delicious.

Minestrone

1 cup macaroni	1 tablespoon butter
1 cup thinly sliced vegetables	1½ pints water
(tomatoes, celery, carrots, onions)	sprig parsley
bay leaf, thyme, salt/pepper	grated Romano cheese

Sauté vegetables in butter. Add other ingredients and boil 2 minutes. Simmer until vegetables are "al dente." Serve with sprinkle of grated cheese.

Eggplant Parmesan

Slice eggplant about ¼ inch thick. Dip in beaten egg to which a bit of basil, oregano or other seasoning has been added. Sauté in butter and sprinkle with Parmesan cheese. Serve hot.

Refried Beans

Boil beans until tender. Mash and refry with onions and oil (canola, soy or olive).

Roasted Grain Coffee

Toast wheat, rye or barley in pan. Grind and use like regular coffee.

Cost Analysis, Vegetarian One

	Cost in cents	Cooked Weight (ounces)
Breakfast:		
Yogurt	.50	16
Seeds, etc.	.15	1
Toast	.10	3
Honey	.15	2
Butter	.12	1
Total	1.02	23
Lunch:		
Veggies	.24	8
Butter	.06	0.5
Parsley	--	2
Bay Leaf	--	--
Thyme	.02	--
Salt	.01	--
Macaroni	.14	16
Romano cheese	.10	0.5
Total	.57	27
Dinner:		
Eggplant	.89	16
Beans	.08	8
Grain coffee	.02	16
Dates	.30	2
Total	1.29	42
Grand Totals	2.88	92

Vegetarian Menu Two

Breakfast: Sliced bananas, Scotch toast with honey, Chamomile tea

Lunch: Barley mushroom soup, Raw carrot sticks, Raspberry tea

Dinner: Zucchini Frittata, Baked potato with yogurt and chives, Spinach and sprout salad with oil, vinegar and home grown basil, Wild clover tea

Scotch Toast with Honey

Beat one egg per person with 1 tablespoon milk. Spread about ½ cup rolled oats on platter. Dip whole wheat bread in egg mixture then dip both sides in the oats. Fry slowly in butter. Two slices per person with honey filling.

Barley Mushroom Soup

Cook $1/4$ cup barley in 1 cup water until tender. Cook 1 grated carrot, 1 sliced onion, $1/8$ lb. sliced mushrooms in oil or butter until tender. Combine with barley and 1 cup vegetable water or stock and add sea salt to taste, finely minced home-grown parsley, and a sprinkle of paprika for color and flavor.

Zucchini Frittata

2 medium zucchini, sliced	1 clove garlic
1 small onion minced	Parmesan cheese

Sauté above in olive oil. Remove from pan. Beat 2 eggs with salt and pepper to taste. Fold in 2 tablespoons Parmesan cheese and the cooked vegetables. Heat oil in skillet and cook mixture, turning carefully until light brown. Serve immediately.

This is tasty vegetarian fare that will make it hard to return to expensive, heavy, acid-forming meat-based meals. Note how liberal your menus can be if you don't pay those high prices for small amounts of meat and poultry. Further, this type of food is easy to digest; you don't have that fagged out feeling after lunch or dinner. Minerals and vitamins of the organic, natural kind abound in fresh-cooked or raw food such as this.

Chapter Eleven
Sample 99¢ Menus

Note to superthrifty chefs: You can buy spices and herbs by the ounce at many natural food stores. This is much cheaper than buying them in packaged form.

Cost Analysis, Vegetarian Two

	Cost in cents	Cooked Weight (ounces)
Breakfast:		
Bananas	.25	8
Scotch Toast	.50	10
Camomile Tea	.10	8
Honey	.08	1
Total	*.93*	27
Lunch:		
Barley	.05	10
Carrot	.13	4
Onion	.05	4
Mushrooms	.24	2
Parsley	--	1
Seasonings	.10	1
Raspberry tea	.10	8
Total	*.67*	30
Dinner:		
Zucchini	.24	8
Onion	.05	4
Garlic	.05	1
Potatoes	.10	8
Yogurt	.15	4
Chives	--	--
Spinach	.10	2
Sprouts	.05	3
Oil	.05	1
Vinegar	.04	1
Home grown basil	--	--
Wild clover tea	--	8
Total	*.83*	40
Grand Totals	**2.43**	**97**

Mineral-Rich Seafood Menu One

Breakfast: Scrambled eggs with herbs, Hot biscuits and honey/butter, Catnip tea (makes humans purr too)

Lunch: Toasted cheese sandwiches, Celery sticks, Fruit in season

Dinner: Sliced tomato and watercress salad, Squid Italienne, Baked squash, Chicory coffee, Wild apples

Squid Italienne

First a word about squid. Most people feel repulsed by anything resembling an octopus, which squid does. However, cleaned, sliced and simmered in a rich Italian sauce, squid competes with the most delicate scallops, shrimp, or other sea food. We ask only that you defer judgment until you make this recipe and try it. Further, with seafood of conventional types out of sight pricewise, squid often becomes quite attractive to both purse and palate.

½ pound squid (must be fresh)
pinch oregano
1 cup solid pack tomatoes
   or equivalent fresh
2 cloves garlic

4 tablespoons olive oil
1 tablespoon chopped
   parsley
dash sherry, optional
salt and pepper to taste

Clean squid and cut into small pieces. Wash well. Pour olive oil in pan and heat. Brown garlic, add squid, sauté about 15 minutes. Add seasonings and cook five minutes longer. Add vegetables and cover. Simmer gently about 10 minutes more or until all is tender and delicious. Serve hot over rice, spaghetti or other pasta if desired.

Cost Analysis, Seafood One

	Cost in cents	Cooked Weight (ounces)
Breakfast:		
Eggs (2)	.20	4
Herbs	.02	--
Flour	.16	12
Shortening	.10	3
Tea	--	8
Total	.48	27
Lunch:		
Rye Bread (2)	.10	3
Cheese	.50	4
Celery	.20	6
Fruit	.25	8
Total	1.05	21
Dinner:		
Tomato	.35	8
Watercress	.08	2
Squid	.65	16
Squash	.11	6
Chicory coffee	--	8
Wild apples	--	8
Total	1.19	48
Grand Totals	**2.72**	**96**

Mineral Rich Seafood Menu Two

Breakfast: Potato pancakes, Baked apple, Wild sassafras tea

Lunch: Broiled soyburgers, Banana spice bars, Lemonade

Dinner: Seafood chowder, Easy bread, Fresh peach cobbler, Black tea or homemade grain coffee

Potato Pancakes

Grate two large potatoes. Blend with 2 tablespoons minced onions, one teaspoon minced parsley, one beaten egg, dash salt, if desired. Form into round patties, fry slowly in oil or butter until browned. Serves two.

Seafood Chowder

Cut about one pound of any low-cost fish into 2-inch pieces. Put into pot and add 1 cup cold water. Bring slowly to boil and cook 5 minutes. Simmer a small sliced onion in oil and add two sliced potatoes. Pour in one-half cup water and cook 10 minutes. Add fish in its liquor, 1 cup scalded milk, and salt and pepper. Simmer another 5 minutes and serve.

Peach Cobbler

(See recipe for blackberry cobbler in Chapter Four and substitute peaches.)

If you live close to a body of water, fish may be free for the catching. If so, your overall costs are that much lower. Again, it is important to discover as many sources of free and wild foods as possible. For example, close to where we are winding up this book, there are many spring salad materials in the open fields, items such as poke, wild radish, dandelion, nettles (steam the tender young leaves). We also observe lots of blackberry vines that will produce later in the summer.

Cost Analysis, Seafood Two

	Cost in cents	Cooked Weight (ounces)
Breakfast:		
Potato pancakes	.50	18
Baked apple	.--	12
Tea	--	10
Total	*.50*	*40*
Lunch:		
Soyburgers	.69	16
Banana bars	.20	6
Lemonade	.10	8
Total	*.99*	*30*
Dinner:		
Seafood chowder	.46	16
Easy bread	.20	6
Peach cobbler	.38	10
Tea	.10	8
Total	*1.14*	*40*
Grand Totals	**2.63**	**110**

Round-The-World Menus for Two

Breakfast: Wild blackberry pancakes (Refer to Western pancake recipe on page 109, add blackberries in abundance), Birch syrup, Homemade grain coffee

Lunch: English Cheese Pudding (Recipes in Chapter Fifteen), Poke salad, Peach Crisp

Dinner: Mexican Hash (Recipe on page 145), Homemade salsa, Spearmint tea and cookies

Birch Syrup

Drill holes in birches, insert hollow tube. Drain sap into buckets. Boil proceeds into thin syrup.

Poke Salad

Gather wild poke greens, add favorite dressing, enjoy.

Peach Crisp

Spread layer of fresh sliced peaches in bottom of pie pan. Sprinkle with mixture of oats, fresh ground whole wheat flour and butter. Dot with more butter and dribble a bit of honey on it. Bake until it bubbles and topping is brown.

Homemade Salsa

Combine chopped tomatoes, onions and green chiles.

Cost Analysis, Round-The-World Menu For Two

		Cost in cents	Cooked Weight (ounces)
Breakfast:			
Berry pancakes		.37	16
Birch syrup		--	4
Grain coffee		.02	8
	Total	.39	28
Lunch:			
Cheese puddin'		.57	12
Tomato		.18	4
Oil & vinegar		.09	2
Peach crisp		.52	16
	Total	1.36	34
Dinner:			
Mexican hash		.76	16
Tomato		.18	4
Onion		.05	4
Green chiles		.20	4
Spearmint tea		--	8
	Total	1.19	36
Grand Totals		2.94	98

Chapter Twelve

Enjoy Better Bread

By Making Your Own

> **What You'll Learn:**
>
> How to win friends and influence people
> with your homebaked bread.

Once you've baked your own bread, you won't want to go back to store-bought plastic foam ever again. The fun and joy of creating something good to eat with your own hands will more than compensate you for the time and effort expended. And there are other bonus benefits:

- Bread made from freshly ground whole wheat flour contains none of the phony chemicals and "enrichments" found in store-bought bread (In a recently conducted test by a Texas biologist, commercial "enriched" bread was fed to weanling

rats for ninety days. All the rats died before the tests were complete.)
- Homemade bread is a simple, healthy combination of natural ingredients — whole grain flour, natural yeast, salt and perhaps some raisins, nuts, or other ingredients to give it texture, flavor and interest.
- The heavier texture of homemade bread requires thorough chewing which helps to clean teeth, stimulate gums, and improve digestion.
- Natural flours give the bread sweetness and goodness not found in the factory-made product.
- By the pound, homemade bread is much less expensive than store-bought bread.
- By using natural leavening such as sourdough or yeast, you avoid chemical baking powders.

Making your own bread can be fun for the whole family. To begin, acquire a sack of whole wheat — any type that pleases you. While you're at it, buy some oats, barley, rye or corn to have around for bread variations.

Whole **G**rain **B**read
Makes 1 5"x 10" loaf

4 cups whole wheat flour, freshly ground
$1^{1}/_{3}$ cups and 3 tablespoons lukewarm water
1 teaspoon salt (optional)

1½ cakes yeast (fresh or dry)
2 tablespoons honey
3 tablespoons oil and melted shortening

Preheat oven to 375°. Dissolve yeast in 3 tablespoons lukewarm water. Add to it the $1^{1}/_{3}$ cups of water, honey, and salt (if desired). Combine with flour. Add the oil or melted shortening. Knead the dough until it is smooth. Shape it into a ball. Cover with cloth and permit to rise for 1 hour. Knead gently once more. Now shape into a loaf and place in greased pan. Let rise again for 1 hour. Bake at 375° for about 50 minutes, or until brown on top.

Salt-Rising Bread
This favorite old-time recipe makes 3 loaves.

1 cup corn meal, freshly ground
1 cup scalded milk
3 cups skim milk
10 to 11 cups whole wheat flour, freshly ground

½ teaspoon salt
1 tablespoon honey
5 tablespoons oil

Preheat oven to 350°. Pour scalded milk over corn meal. Permit this to ferment in a warm place for about 12 hours. Mix skim milk, salt, honey, and oil (sesame is great for this) and heat mixture until lukewarm. Stir in three cups of whole wheat flour and add corn mixture. Place in warm place for 2 to 3 hours. Next, stir in 5 more cups whole wheat flour. Knead until smooth, adding another 2 to 3 cups whole wheat flour. Place the dough in three greased pans and allow it to set until it has doubled in bulk. Bake at 350° for 1 hour or until done. Cool and slice.

Quick and Easy Bread

2 tablespoons honey
4 large eggs
½ cup butter or oil
2 cups whole wheat flour

pinch of salt
2 cakes yeast (fresh or dry)
3 tablespoons warm milk or water

Preheat oven to 425°. Beat honey with eggs. Add butter or oil, flour and salt. Dissolve the yeast in warm milk or water. Add these items to the batter and beat it briskly for a couple of minutes. Place in a greased bread loaf pan and let the dough rise in a warm place for about 3 hours. Bake at 425° for about 30 minutes or until brown.

Boston Brown Bread

1 cup freshly ground corn meal
1 cup freshly ground rye flour
1 cup graham flour
¾ teaspoon soda

½ teaspoon salt (optional)
2 cups sour milk
¾ cup molasses
1 cup chopped raisins

Combine the meal, flours, soda and salt. In a separate bowl mix liquid ingredients and raisins. Add to dry ingredients. Pour batter into a buttered 2-quart pudding mold and steam for 3 to 4 hours. May be steamed in smaller molds or baking powder cans for 1½ to 2 hours.

Wheat Berry Batter Bread

2¼ cups unsifted flour
1 tablespoon honey
¾ tsp. salt
1 pkg. dry yeast
1 cup lukewarm water
Melted butter

½ cup cooked wheat
  berries
1 tablespoon butter
  (melted)
Corn meal

In a bowl, combine 1½ cups of flour, honey, salt and yeast. Gradually beat in the warm water. Beat at medium speed for 3 minutes or until dough is elastic. Add wheat. Gradually beat in remaining ¾ cups flour at low speed; the dough should be very soft and elastic.

Cover and let stand in a warm place until doubled, about 45 minutes. Stir down dough. Grease a 4 x 8 inch pan and coat with corn meal. Spoon dough into pan. Bake at 375° for about 1 hour or until a skewer inserted in the center of the loaf comes out clean and crust is well browned. Brush top with melted butter. Makes 1 loaf.

By the way, all breads can be made into rolls. Simply break off chunks of dough and shape them into roll form. Add nuts, raisins,

Chapter Twelve
Enjoy Better Bread By Making Your Own

seeds and other goodies to produce a variety of freshly baked good things.

THE "RIPE" TEST   KNEADING   PUNCHING DOWN THE DOUGH

Steps in shaping a loaf of bread

CRESCENTS

CLOVERLEAF

FAN TANS

PARKERHOUSE

Chapter Thirteen

The Noble Spud To Your Budget's Rescue

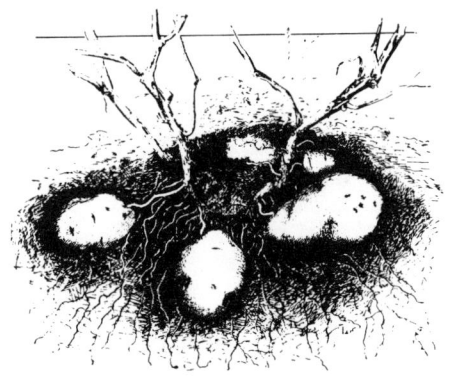

> **What You'll Learn:**
> One of the secrets of living on meals that cost pennies instead of dollars: new ways of preparing low cost foods. Here's all the information you need to make the noble potato a thing of great beauty and special taste.

For the money spent, potatoes give consumers a high return in food value. One medium-sized potato, boiled, baked, or pressure-cooked can supply:

- one-fourth of the Vitamin C recommended for an adult each day
- worthwhile amounts of thiamin and niacin (B vitamins)
- substantial quantities of iron and potassium.

The potato is a healthy food, and it's no more calories than an apple, orange, or banana. For example, a potato of medium size, boiled or baked provides only about a hundred calories. The commonly added fats, gravies, and sauces are the things that make potatoes an offender for those who must watch their weight as well as their food dollars. Fried potatoes, for example, are the fat cats of the spud tribe. They may be two to four times as high in calories as the same weight of boiled, baked, or pressure-cooked potatoes. So don't blame potatoes for that tight dress or belt. Treat them kindly and plainly and you'll stay healthy and slender.

Buying Potatoes

The best potatoes are firm, smooth and well-shaped. They are free from cuts, blemishes and decay. Look for potatoes that are reasonably clean so you can see if there are green spots. Avoid this type since the green parts are bitter. If you intend to buy a large quantity at one time, it's very important that you cook and taste a few potatoes from the batch before making your purchase.

Storing Spuds

Potatoes will keep for several months if stored in a cool place with good ventilation. Sort through them and remove any that are cut or blemished. Use these first since they will probably be the first to spoil.

The ideal storage place is in a dark space with a temperature of around 40 to 45° F. A cellar is perfect, but be sure and avoid dampness.

Cooking Potatoes

Don't peel potatoes; if you do you lose the best part, since most of the vitamins and minerals are near the surface. Cook them

Chapter Thirteen
The Noble Spud To Your Budget's Rescue

fast in a small amount of water if you like them boiled; quick cooking saves the nutritional elements. Baking is an even better way to prepare them. Scrub them thoroughly so that the skins can be eaten without fear of dirt.

Eating well on a low budget never need be a drab, colorless, and tasteless way to live. Actually the finest meals in the world are usually the simplest ones — a melted cheese sandwich and German potato salad, or a fresh green salad with potatoes au gratin. Here are some great ways to make spuds stand by themselves, even as main dishes.

There are better ways to cook potatoes than frying them. Here are some examples:

Red Onion Potato Salad

6 medium spuds, peeled, cooked, and sliced
¼ cup chopped parsley
3 tablespoons wine vinegar
Dash cayenne pepper or splash of hot sauce

¼ cup Italian dressing
1 cup each, chopped celery and sweet red onion

Combine hot potatoes with other ingredients. Serve immediately to hot potato lovers or chill for later use.

Potato Dumplings

2 cups mashed potatoes made with skim milk
1 egg
¼ cup whole wheat flour, freshly ground
1 heaping tablespoon each, minced onion, parsley

Mix well and add by teaspoonfuls to hot stew or soup. Simmer 20 minutes.

Spud and Carrot Bash

This is one of our favorite vegetarian meals and has been for many decades. Must be good since our combined ages now total more than a century and a half!

3 large spuds, chopped into walnut-size pieces for quick cooking
3 large carrots, same as above
¼ cup olive oil
½ teaspoon each of cumin, paprika and basil (or your favorite spices to taste)
¼ cup chopped raw sweet onion
Splash or two of soy sauce or shoyu.

Boil spuds and carrots until tender. Drain, mash and add other ingredients. Mix well and serve immediately.

Topped Spuds

An even simpler method of enjoying freshly cooked spuds is to steam, boil or bake them and then top with any of the following:

Vinaigrette dressing, vinegar and a dash of olive oil. Balsamic vinegar makes this a special treat.
Dijon mustard with a dash of sour cream

Chapter Thirteen
The Noble Spud To Your Budget's Rescue

Yogurt embellished with your favorite herbs and a splash of white wine.
Toasted sesame seeds.
Whipped butter and dash of poppy seeds.
Slivered pimiento and green pepper.
Melted butter thinned with lemon juice.
Sliced mushrooms marinated in your favorite dressing.
Grated Parmesan and/or Romano cheese.
Chopped onion with paprika and coarsely ground black pepper.
Chives and cottage cheese or yogurt.
...let your imagination roam and you'll never be bored with spuds.

Skinny French Fries

Cooking in deep fat is not healthy but you can use a little non-hydrogenated, cold-pressed oil to make these replicas of french fries in your oven.

4 medium potatoes, peeled and cut in strips
2 tablespoons oil
Salt and paprika to taste

Chill strips in ice water to crisp. Drain and dry. Spread strips in one layer on pan. Sprinkle with oil and shake pan to distribute oil evenly. Bake at 450° F until golden brown and tender, about 40 minutes. Turn frequently. Sprinkle salt/paprika to taste.

Chapter Fourteen

Soybeans: The Money-Saving Meat Substitute

What You'll Learn:
Why the Chinese have been using soybeans for centuries, and how you can do it too. The economics and dietetics of soybeans in summary form.

Of all the many adventures we've enjoyed, one of the most educational was the ownership of a 75-foot former Coast Guard cutter converted to a floating home. We lived on it off and on for more than seven years in all kinds of odd waterfront locations.

One of the best was a tie-up to Bradford Island in the California Delta where we invited a number of homeless people to join us for an experiment in alternative lifestyles. With no rent to pay, the major expenditure of our limited funds was for food.

Soybeans became a staunch staple appearing in such popular forms as soy chili and the all-time favorite, soy burgers. The recipe for this gem appears shortly.

As much of our shipboard diet was vegetarian, the protein from soy was important for nutritional balance. And since this revision has an even stronger vegan orientation than the original edition, it's vital that protein sources be revealed.

> "The soybean is in so many respects the most valuable of all plant foods." — United States Office of Health Education

About the closest most Americans have come to soybeans is the adding of a little soy sauce to the chow mein at Ah Sing's Oriental Gardens. Good, wasn't it? The soybean is even better when you become familiar with its fantastic versatility. In fact, it's better from many standpoints — economic, nutrition, convenience, and taste.

First, some facts. Soy plants are defined in botanical languages as a small erect herb (Glycine soja) that grows in many parts of the world but primarily in China, India and the United States. The plant itself makes excellent forage for animals, while from the human's point of view, its bean is a source of oil, flour and hundreds of other products.

Here are just a few of the ways in which soybeans are used in the home as food: green soybeans, fresh or frozen; soy flour; soy grits; soy milk; dry soybeans; canned green soybeans; soybean pulp, and the ever-popular soy sauce.

Proximate Analysis of Soy Flour

Composition	Full-fat soy flour per cent	Defatted soy flour per cent
Protein	41.0	50.5
Fat	20.5	1.5
Carbohydrates	25.2	34.2

Chapter Fourteen
Soybeans: The Money-Saving Meat Substitute

The soybean is the only vegetable that yields a complete protein comparable in quality to that of milk, eggs, and meat. Soybeans also consist of about 20 percent unsaturated fats, the most important of these being lecithin, which is also a constituent of eggs, nuts, and seeds. Lecithin has the ability to break up cholesterol and other fatty substances in the body so that they are discouraged from forming plaques within the artery walls.

Soy Protein Manufacturer

COMPANY	PRODUCT NAME	PRODUCT FORM
Loma Linda Foods	Fibrotein and TVP (Textured vegetable protein)	Dry and canned soy protein
Worthington Foods (Miles Laboratory)	Fibrotein	Dry, frozen and canned soy protein
General Mills, Inc.	Bacos Bontrae	Dry soy protein Frozen soy protein
Archer Daniels	TVP	Dry soy protein
*A.E. Stanley Co.	Mira-Tex	
*Central Soya	Promosoy	
*Farm-Mar-Co.	Ultra-Soy	
*H.B. Taylor Co.	Textra Soy	
*Ralston Purina	Edi-Pro	
*Swift and Co.	Texgran	

*Companies that make several soy protein ingredients but do not market any as "finished" products to use in recipes.

Cost

Besides their nutritional value, the most outstanding feature of soybeans is their low cost both in terms of price per pound and price per unit of food value. Take a look at this comparison of soybeans and beef:

4½ pounds **Beef** (rib roast)	$10.00	25 pounds **Soybeans**
	Mrs. Smith Received:	
from beef		from soybeans
6	Servings	150
13	Days Protein	180
355	Total Protein (gm)	4,540
5,659	Calories	37,569
204	Calcium (mg)	25,756
3,841	Phosphorus (mg)	66,511
53	Iron (mg)	908
0	Vitamin A (I.U.)	15,890
2	Vitamin B1 (mg)	121
3	Vitamin B2 (mg)	35

By using soybeans, then, you get *25 times* more servings (6 of beef to 150 of soybeans!), *13 times* more protein, about *seven times* the calories, and very big jolts of valuable vitamins. Think of how much better your entire family will feel when they add soybeans to their diet. You'll be able to tell the difference in a matter of days. In addition, you'll need a haybaler to wire up the dollars you'll save by not buying beef.

Many cookbooks neglect this important food, so we'll make up the deficit right now.

Soy Burgers

Soak 1 cup dry soybeans overnight and cook covered over low heat for 2 to 3 hours or until tender. Drain off liquid (stock can be used for soups), mash very well, and add any of the following, experimenting with different amounts of combinations: chopped onions, chopped (fine) garlic, celery, sesame seeds, sunflower seeds, chopped green pepper, cooked brown rice or bulgar wheat, chopped fresh parsley.

Make into patties and broil until browned. Serve on whole wheat buns or bread with homemade mayonnaise and plenty of alfalfa sprouts.

Soybean Soufflé

3 cups soybean pulp
3 eggs, separated
1 tablespoon chopped onion

2 tablespoons chopped parsley
salt and pepper to taste

To make the pulp, drain cooked soybeans. Put through a food press or sieve, or mash thoroughly. This paste may be stored in the refrigerator and used as needed.

Preheat oven to 325°. Beat the yolks of the eggs and add them to the other ingredients. Then fold this mixture into the well-beaten egg whites, and pour into a greased baking dish. Bake at 325° for 30 minutes or until set. Serve at once.

Honey Soy Drink

1 cup soy milk powder
4 cups water

1 tablespoon honey

Mix powder with a small amount of water until smooth. Blend into remaining water. Let stand 2 hours. Cook 20 minutes in double boiler. Strain. Flavor with honey and salt. Keep refrigerated.

I believe that Bill Shurtleff and his wife Akiko have done more to eliminate hunger on earth than any other couple. They have devoted their lives to the acquisition and transmittal of information on soy by establishing the Soy Center. When I started to summarize their incredible accomplishments I realized it would require a book. Much simpler and compact is the presentation of the *Chronology of the Center* which will greatly expand your knowledge of this marvelous foodstuff.

For more information, send a large SASE to the address on the following page. You'll be enlightened; we guarantee it.

Chapter Fourteen
Soybeans: The Money-Saving Meat Substitute

Soyfoods Center

The World's Leading Source of Information on Soyfoods

Founded 1976 ■ SoyaScan Databases ■ Publishing ■ Consulting ■ Research Library

ABOUT THE SOYFOODS CENTER

In October 1972, the founders of the Soyfoods Center, William Shurtleff and Akiko Aoyagi Shurtleff, started full-time research on soyfoods in Japan. Their first book, *The Book of Tofu*, was published in December 1975, and in August 1976 they formally founded the Soyfoods Center. Today the Center is the world's leading source of information in this rapidly growing new field.

Shurtleff and Aoyagi have written thirteen books (including popular books, technical manuals, market studies, and histories), published 38 extensive bibliographies, and compiled 7 volumes in a series titled *Soyfoods Marketing: Labels, Ads, Posters, and Other Graphics*. These works have sold more than 585,000 copies to date. They have been widely credited with starting the soyfoods movement in the Western world and creating a new industry.

The Center also has a library of 35,000 documents, and produces three computerized databases. The largest of these, SoyaScan Publications, is a bibliographic database listing more than 42,500 documents on soybeans and soyfoods from 1100 B.C. to the present. More than half of all records contain a substantial summary. SoyaScan Products gives details on more than 10,100 commercial soyfood products from 1546 A.D. to the present, and SoyaScan Directory and Mailing List contains over 12,500 soy-related names and addresses.

Their best-selling *Book of Tofu* and *Tofu & Soymilk Production*, and their active Soyfoods Consulting Service, have helped in the establishment of more than 250 companies making tofu and tofu products in America alone, and a $150 million industry.

The Soyfoods Center's work has three main purposes:

1. To introduce soyfoods to the Western world. Of special interest are tofu (the world's most popular food made from soya), soymilk, soy ice creams, yogurts, and cheeses, tempeh, miso, soy sauce, soy flour, fresh green soybeans, soynuts, soy sprouts, yuba, and natto. These have served as the protein backbone of the diet for one quarter of the world's people in East Asia for more than 1,000 years.

2. To provide a meatless alternative to standard American meat-centered standard American diet, which is a major factor behind the shocking statistics that 50 percent of all Americans die of coronary heart disease and another 20 percent die of cancer.

3. To do something about world hunger and world protein shortages. During the past decade, roughly 20 million people a year have died of hunger and malnutrition-related diseases. Three quarters of these are children. Yet there is plenty of food today in the world for everyone. In America, for example, one half of all our agricultural land is used to grow crops that are fed to animals.

P.O. Box 234, Lafayette, CA 94549-0234 USA ■ Phone: (510) 283-2991 ■ Fax: (510) 283-9091
(For UPS and Express Mail only: 1021 Dolores Dr.)

Printed on Recycled Paper 30% Postconsumer Content

Chapter Fifteen

Recipes From

Around The World

What You'll Learn:

That a variety of taste-tempting, low-cost foods are available at your local ethnic specialty grocery. How to go the foreign-food route to eat better for less. Recipes and specifics.

NOTE: In the attempt to reprice these ethnic dishes it became apparent that there were too many variables. Any price we assigned could be changed by the seasons, whether the cook grew some or all of the ingredients, whether basics were purchased in bulk and so forth.

For example, if the cost of each recipe were based on our lifestyle for a period in the 70s, they would be so low as to be unbelievable. I recall that we were able to live for about *25¢ per person per day for EVERYTHING* while aboard our ship. However, this was due to our growing or finding almost all of our food and having no rent or utilities to pay.

This basic principle... the pursuit of a low-cost, fulfilling lifestyle will allow one to live high on a low budget. In short, *eating well for less is basically a lifestyle choice.*

Most American communities have at least one small ethnic grocery store, and the larger cities often have a store for each racial and ethnic group — Mexican, Chinese, Italian, Japanese, and so forth. Even tiny towns often have a store that caters to a specific segment of the population. For example, there's a store in Soledad, California, a village just off the north-south freeway, that sells every conceivable Mexican foodstuff and fresh hot tamales that I can't pass up, even on the most urgent trip up or down the state. So look around your own community. Check the phone book under grocers; if you see a Juanita's Grocery or a Pasquale's Produce, drop in soon. Buy things like:

- Tortillas, 40¢ a dozen
- Tamales (you can make your own), varies
- Masa (corn flour), 25¢ a pound
- Dried Hot Chiles, $1.20 & up per pound
- Mexican cheese, $1.50 per pound
- Pinto beans, 50¢ per pound

(These are current 1995 prices.)

The recipes that follow are intended to introduce you to the world's store of culinary skill and imagination. Most of the dishes presented do not require specialty foods, and can be prepared from the foods you would ordinarily have on hand in your pantry and storage bins.

Chapter Fifteen
Recipes From Around The World

Mexican Food

Mexico, despite the tourist advertising you read, is a very poor country. The majority of its population lives only slightly above subsistence level. This has always been so and conditions change slowly, so the average Mexican has had lots of time to learn how to make very plain and simple foods taste delicious. The proliferation of Mexican restaurants in the United States attests to the popularity of Mexican food. Of all ethnic foods, I believe that Mexican foods offer the most taste for the least amount of money. Here are several Mexican dishes that anyone can make.

Mexican Hash

2 large onions, chopped
Salt to taste
2 teaspoons olive oil
2 cups cooked kidney beans

2 teaspoons chili powder
¼ teaspoon pepper
2 cups shredded lettuce

Sauté chopped onions in oil, add chili, salt, pepper, and beans. Cook slowly for 15 minutes, stirring occasionally. Serve on deep platter with shredded lettuce piled in mound in center. Salsa optional, but good. Serves 4. (Salsa usually consists of chopped tomatoes, onions and green chiles in any desired proportions.)

Huevos Rancheros

Make a hot ranchero sauce by combining tomato sauce with sautéed onions, peppers (green or red), and a bit of chili powder. This is a freewheeling type of sauce; you can toss into it anything with a Mexican bent. When bubbling, break some eggs into the sauce and poach them. Serve with hot buttered tortillas.

Refried Beans

Soak some pinto or red kidney beans overnight. Rinse and check for rocks. Simmer until tender. Drain, combine with sautéed onions, as many green chiles as you can afford, and a fair quantity of quality oil. Now they can be reheated (refried) at any time as a delicious side dish to any other Mexican treat.

Tacos

A close friend of mine solved the problem of ensuring a good diet for his eight children. He simply let them go wild on infinite variations of tacos. The tortillas are usually quite cheap and the fillings can be anything; lettuce, cheese and sauce to beans, rice, chopped crisp vegetables of all kinds and homemade dressings.

I've often eaten at this household, and never got the same type of taco twice; I was never disappointed.

Try this low-cost, healthy way to feeding a bunch. Here's the basic taco recipe... the fillings can be varied to suit what you have or what you like: Heat tortillas in frying pan in hot oil. Fold over and fry until as crisp as desired. Then fill with cheese, beans, rice, chiles, lettuce, tomatoes, olives, avocados, any or all. Top with hot sauce or salsa, if desired.

Chowders

So you think there are only two kinds of clam chowder — Boston, the white kind, and Manhattan, with the tomato base? Well, my friend from Baja reports that down on his peninsula chowder is made from just about anything that swims: codfish, mussel, goose barnacle, oyster, sea bass, and shrimp.

Italian Food

As food costs rise, the Italian genius for making blah pasta taste divine with slow simmered sauces becomes ever more valuable. You can develop this skill in your own kitchen. But Italian cooking involves more than just pasta. Here's an introductory assortment of recipes.

Chapter Fifteen
Recipes From Around The World

Italian Gnocchi

2 cups milk
½ cup farina
1 teaspoon salt

2 tablespoons butter
1 cup grated cheese
2 eggs

Preheat oven to 375°. Scald the milk in the top of a double boiler. Gradually add the farina; cook and stir until the mixture thickens. Add the salt and butter and continue to cook for 20 minutes, stirring occasionally. Remove from the heat; add the cheese, and stir until the mixture is free from lumps. Separate the eggs; beat the yolks until thick and lemon-colored; and add to the farina mixture. Fold in the egg whites, whipped stiff; and transfer mixture to a shallow-loaf cake pan, rinsed with cold water. Cool, chill, and cut in squares, rounds, fancy shapes with sandwich cutters. Transfer to a shallow pan rubbed plentifully with butter, sprinkle with the additional cheese. Bake in a hot oven, 375°, for 15 minutes, or until brown all over.

Italian Spaghetti

1 pound uncooked spaghetti
½ cup butter
3 cloves garlic or ½ cup chopped raw onion
1 can tomato paste
Add oregano, thyme or any other appropriate spices

water
¾ teaspoon salt
¼ teaspoon pepper
Parmesan cheese

Boil the spaghetti until tender but not mushy in salted water. Drain. While the spaghetti is cooking put the butter in a small heavy frying pan; add the garlic or onion, and sauté. Combine the tomato paste with an equal amount of water; add garlic/onion and simmer until thick; season with the salt and pepper. Allow 30 minutes to make this sauce. Pour over the spaghetti and top with plenty of Parmesan cheese.

Italian Eggplant

1 medium-sized eggplant	¼ cup grated Parmesan
flour, whole wheat	salt and pepper
2 eggs	2 tablespoons minced
2 tablespoons butter	parsley
2 cups canned tomatoes	pinch of oregano, sage, thyme or basil

Preheat oven to 350°. Slice the eggplant in quarter-inch slices. It is not necessary to peel it or to squeeze out the juice. Dip each slice in flour. Slightly beat the eggs and add the cheese, one-fourth teaspoon black pepper, one-half teaspoon salt, and the parsley. Dip the floured slices in this mixture and fry first on one side then on the other until browned in butter. Remove the eggplant. Add the tomato and simmer ten minutes. Then place the eggplant in layers in buttered baking dish and pour the tomato mixture over it. Bake for 20 minutes at 350°.

Chinese Food

The Chinese have the oldest continuous culture on earth, so it's no surprise that their culinary prowess transcends all others. Nor is it surprising that they've discovered how to maintain good health, top taste, and mealtime interest all on a foundation of extremely basic food elements. Practically everything you enjoy in a Chinese restaurant is inexpensive. What meat is used is treated as if it were the crown jewels it now resembles in price. Learn to make your own egg foo yung and chow mein; you'll be pleasantly surprised at how easy it is.

Chapter Fifteen
Recipes From Around The World

Shrimp Egg Foo Yung

2 teaspoons cornstarch
¼ cup water
1 chicken bouillon cube
2 teaspoons soy sauce
¼ teaspoon salt
1 tablespoon oil
1 cup bean sprouts (your own homegrown sprouts)
1 teaspoon vinegar
½ teaspoon honey
6 eggs
1 cup diced shrimp, fresh or frozen
½ cup chopped green onions

Blend cornstarch with water in a pan until smooth, add chicken cube, soy sauce, vinegar, and honey. Cook, stirring constantly until sauce thickens. Keep warm on low heat. Beat eggs in bowl, stir in shrimp, onions, sprouts, and salt. Heat a large old cast iron skillet until water drops dance on its surface. Lightly grease with oil. Pour on egg mixture about 3 tablespoons at a time. Bake until set and turn. Serve with sauce on top.

Flying Goose Chow Mein

One summer, we all stayed on our boat, an old Coast Guard cutter called the Flying Goose. We made lots of Chinese food because it's cheap and healthy. This was one of our favorites.

Cut up and stir fry (quickly fry in oil) a lot of different vegetables, starting with the toughest ones first — celery and onions — and ending up with the tenderest — sprouts and bok choy leaves. In a separate pot, boil up a big quantity of chow mein noodles. These can be purchased in fresh or dry form. Drain noodles, add some sesame oil and mix. Now serve the vegetables over the noodles and pass the soy sauce. Optional, pass the Thailand Fish Soy, which is super great!

Soybeans Shanghai

1 cup cooked soybeans (best to soak overnight, then simmer until tender)	½ cup celery or bok choy, sliced
½ cup of water in which soybeans were cooked	½ onion, grated
	½ cup tomatoes, diced
	¼ cup soy sauce

Simmer ingredients 15 minutes; serve hot with crisp noodles or wonton.

Japanese Food

Similar in many ways to Chinese, Japanese cookery is strong on seafood. After all, besides rice, seafood is the only major food resource in Japan. Once you've tried "raw fish" (actually it is "cooked" by enzyme action), you'll probably (to continue the imagery), be hooked for life.

Sushi (Japanese Raw Fish)

Cube raw fish, marinate in lemon or lime juice one hour or more. Serve chilled with soy sauce or hot mustard and tomato sauce combination. Simple, delicious, nutritious, inexpensive.

German Food

The thought of German cooking often elicits an image of rather heavy food. This is not entirely accurate. The peasant culture has dreamed up some highly creative dishes — for instance, shredded red cabbage flavored with caraway seeds and other spices. This imaginative treatment transforms the cabbage into pure vegetary ambrosia, delicious hot or cold. Best of all, it's cheap. So look for the characteristic dishes in a good German cookbook. Here's a selection I learned by heart from my mother.

Chapter Fifteen
Recipes From Around The World

Potato and Herring Casserole

1 large onion
6 cups raw potatoes
¼ teaspoon pepper

3 tablespoons butter
1 can herring
½ pint cream

Preheat oven to 350°. Sauté onion until soft in 2 tablespoons of butter. Layer potatoes, herring and onion in a large greased baking dish. Begin and end with the spuds. Sprinkle pepper between layers. Pour cream over potatoes. Dot top with remaining butter. Bake covered at 350° for 30 minutes. Remove cover and bake 30 minutes more until bubbling and golden brown.

Red Cabbage

The Chinese serve red cabbage mixed with green peppers and vinegar. But the Germans offer us this delicious combination. It's great hot, and better the next day served as a cold relish.

1 head red cabbage
2 tablespoons olive oil
2 tablespoons onion, chopped
2 apples, cored and sliced thin
caraway seeds

2 tablespoons flour
½ cup diluted vinegar or red wine
2 tablespoons honey

Trim cabbage, cut into sections, remove core, shred and soak in cold water. Sauté chopped onion in oil. Simmer cabbage with ¼ teaspoon salt for about 1½ hours. Add water if necessary and caraway seeds to suit. Dissolve flour in diluted vinegar or red wine, stir in honey and add to cabbage mixture. Simmer 10 or 15 minutes longer. Serves 4.

French Food
Do you know how the doughty, independent French have survived two world wars, Charles de Gaulle, and a declining share

of world markets? It's simple — an unusually large proportion of French families have backyard gardens from which to obtain staples. The vegetables and fruits they grow, and the goats that some have for milk, provide the rudiments of all meals. These items plus some wine, the ubiquitous and rightfully famous French bread, and an occasional rack of lamb would keep any family happy. (We might take this to heart and plant some vegetable seeds instead of lawn come spring.)

Here are two recipes so French that they are almost indecently delicious.

Béarnaise Sauce

3 tablespoons cider vinegar
3 tablespoons tarragon vinegar
1 small onion, minced
$1/8$ teaspoon cayenne

3 egg yolks
½ cup butter
½ teaspoon salt

Combine the vinegars; add the onion and cook for three minutes over a moderate heat. Strain onion out and pour the liquor into the egg yolks, well beaten. Transfer mixture to the top of a double boiler. Cook and stir over a low heat until the mixture thickens. Then add the butter a teaspoonful at a time, working in each portion before more is added. Season with the salt and cayenne and serve immediately over broiled meat or fish. Also delicious over egg dishes.

Steamed French Bread Pudding

1 small loaf bread or 3 cups
   (solidly packed) bread cubes
½ cup butter
½ cup honey
½ teaspoon baking powder

2 eggs
½ teaspoon nutmeg
grated rind of 1 orange
$1/3$ cup chopped raisins
2 tablespoons shredded
   citron (optional)

Chapter Fifteen
Recipes From Around The World

The bread should be cut or broken into very small pieces. In a bowl, pour enough hot water over the bread to barely cover it. Cool, drain, and press as much water out as possible with a fork. In a large bowl cream the butter with the honey and the egg yolks slightly beaten. Add the bread, nutmeg, orange rind, baking powder, raisins, and citron. Fold in the egg whites, stiffly whipped. Transfer to a mold rubbed with butter. Cover tightly, place on a trivet in a pot with 1 inch of boiling water. Cover kettle closely, lower heat, and steam for two hours. Unmold and serve with hard or pineapple sauce.

Middle Eastern Dishes

A teacher friend of mine who had spent some years in Turkey said that the American dollar went further there than in any other place in Europe. That, of course, means that the standard of living in Turkey is low and that foods are, of necessity, cheap and filling. Further, people strive mightily to make the most of what little they have. All of this leads to some interesting recipes for fundamental foods.

Constantinople Meatless Pepper Pot

½ cup garbanzo beans (cow peas)
1½ quarts well-seasoned soup stock, your choice of spices
juice of ½ lemon
salt and pepper
1 egg

6 cloves garlic, crushed, and 2 minced onions
1½ tablespoon flour
1 tablespoon butter
boiled rice

Soak the cow-peas overnight. Drain and add to the stock, which should be boiling. Cook rapidly for an hour. Add garlic to the stock, replenishing the stock as it evaporates. Simmer two hours. Season to taste with salt and pepper. Cream together the butter, flour, and lemon juice. Stir carefully into the soup and boil a minute or two, stirring constantly. Beat the egg lightly with a bit of hot soup and add. Serve at once with large spoonfuls of boiled rice in the center of each plate.

Pilaf

Takes the place of potatoes and is better than anything you buy in a box.

1 cup barley (or any other grain)	1 large onion
4 tablespoons butter	chicken broth

Cook barley in a large amount of boiling water until tender and drain. Sauté onion in butter until soft, stir in chicken broth. Add barley, toss to mix well. Cover. Heat very slowly until heated through. A low cost, tasty dish you'll serve often. Rice and other grains can be adorned in the same way. Serves 2 generously.

Soul Food

In the old days, the masters of plantations ate high on the hog and gave their slaves the leftovers. Necessity being the mother of invention, all those scraps developed into some tasty dishes passed down and refined through the generations.

Soul Succotash

1 cup dried baby lima beans, soaked overnight in refrigerator	2 small bay leaves
3 cups water	1 tablespoon chopped green peppers
1 teaspoon salt	1 tablespoon olive oil
1 can (#303) stewed tomatoes or 2 cups tomatoes with juice	1 cup corn kernels
	¼ teaspoon thyme

Place in a large pot all the ingredients, except the corn. Bring to a boil. Cover pot. Lower heat. Simmer 1½ hours. Add more water, if needed. Water should cover beans and vegetables throughout cooking time. Add corn. Cover. Cook another 25 minutes. Correct seasoning. Serves 4.

Chapter Fifteen
Recipes From Around The World

This recipe is so simple, you'll laugh when you read the directions.

Wild Willy's Corncakes

Grind up a cup or so of your whole grain corn to a reasonably fine texture. Mix into a thin batter with water, milk and even a nice fresh organic egg or two. But water alone will do if you're going the poor-man route. Heat your griddle until a drop of water dances on the surface. Grease the griddle with whatever you have available — butter or oil. Now pour the batter out so it fairly crackles as it solidifies. It should be a quick process; otherwise you'll get soggy little cakes that will just sit there with a mournful expression. A well-cooked corncake is crisp on the edges. They are delicious with butter and whatever else you have available — honey, chopped fresh fruit, ground dates. Be imaginative; roll them up with sour cream and slices of melon or cottage cheese. They make a good substitute for tortillas, too. Great food any time — morning, noon, or night.

Indian Food

People in India, despite news bulletins of disaster and famine, do get something to eat once in a while. And here is an example of what they do with it. You may find the distinctively Indian curry flavor a delicious change. An easy way to add variety to your diet.

Indian Sauce

1½ tablespoon butter
1½ tablespoon flour
1 cup soup stock
1 teaspoon curry powder
a bit of bay leaf
few grains cayenne

½ tablespoon minced onion
grated rind of ¼ lemon
½ cup chopped tomato
few grains salt

Melt the butter. Add the flour and gradually the soup stock. Stir in the curry powder, mixed with a teaspoonful of cold water. Add the remaining ingredients to the sauce and season to taste. Simmer about ten minutes.

Curry Soup

½ pound lentils
2 pints water or stock
2 large onions
1 turnip
1 tablespoon flour, whole wheat

2 tablespoons butter
2 teaspoons curry powder
2 teaspoons chutney
salt and pepper optional

Fry sliced vegetables in butter until brown. Add lentils and water or stock. Simmer one hour; then sieve or blend to smoothness. Return to pan and reheat with flour and seasonings. Serve with chapatties (Indian tortilla-like bread) or crackers.

Swiss Food
Switzerland is famous for more than its beautiful scenery. The Swiss are particularly imaginative when it comes to dairy food.

Swiss Cheese Biscuits

(Can be made with other kinds of cheese, like Cheddar, for example.)

2 cups whole wheat flour
4 teaspoons baking powder
½ teaspoon salt
6 tablespoons butter

2 egg yolks or one whole egg
$^2/_3$ cup milk
½ cup grated Swiss (or other) cheese

Preheat oven to 425°. Sift the dry ingredients together and cut in the butter with the back and edge of a spoon until the consistency of coarse cornmeal. In another bowl beat the egg yolks and add the milk; mix and add to the first mixture and mix until blended. Transfer to board dusted with flour and knead for a few seconds. Roll or pat out to $1/8$ inch in thickness and sprinkle half of the dough with the grated cheese. Fold the dough over and shape with a small biscuit cutter. Transfer to a shallow pan or baking sheet rubbed with butter. Brush the tops of the biscuits with a little milk and sprinkle with a little additional cheese. Bake in a very hot oven 400-425° for 15 minutes, or until puffy and brown.

Danish Food

Danish pastries and cheese dishes are world-famous.

Danish Apfelskiver

1½ cups whole wheat flour
2 teaspoons baking powder
½ teaspoon salt

3 eggs, separated
1 cup milk
3 tablespoons melted butter

Preheat oven to 375°. Sift the dry ingredients. In a separate bowl, beat the egg yolks and add the milk. Stir into the flour mixture; add the butter and egg whites, whipped stiff. Transfer to hot Apfelskiver pans rubbed with butter or use tiny round muffin pans. Bake about 20 minutes at 375°. Adorn with applesauce.

Rich Cheese Sauce

4 tablespoons butter
3 tablespoons whole wheat flour
½ teaspoon salt

¼ teaspoon paprika
1½ cups milk
1 cup finely chopped sharp cheddar

Melt the butter, add the flour and seasonings, and blend. Gradually add the milk. Cook and stir until the sauce thickens. Add the cheese. Place over hot water, or in the top of a double boiler and cook and stir until the cheese melts.

Scottish Food

The independent Scottish people draw much of their sustenance from rough and nutritious grains. Here are a couple of appropriate recipes.

Plain Scones

2 cups whole wheat flour
1 tablespoon honey
¼ teaspoon baking soda
½ teaspoon salt

2½ teaspoons baking powder
5 tablespoons butter
¾ cup buttermilk or sour milk

Preheat oven to 400°. Sift the dry ingredients together. Cut in the butter until the consistency of coarse cornmeal. Add the buttermilk, blend the mixture together, and divide into two portions. Transfer to a board dusted with flour; and roll each portion into a round shape, ¼ inch in thickness. Cut each round in quarters, and transfer to a baking sheet generously rubbed with butter. Bake at 400° for 15 minutes, or until brown on top. Split, spread with butter, and serve hot with marmalade or jam.

Scotch Shortbread

2 cups whole wheat flour
½ teaspoon salt
½ teaspoon nutmeg

¾ cup butter
½ cup honey

Preheat oven to 350°. Sift together the flour, salt and nutmeg. Rub the butter into dry ingredients with the finger tips; then work in the honey, continually kneading and working until the dough is smooth and feels like pastry. Transfer to a square pan lined with waxed paper, pressing it out to a ¾ inch thickness. Bake at 350 to 375° for 30 minutes. Cut in small squares when half cooled; and remove from the pan.

Chapter Fifteen
Recipes From Around The World

English Food

It's not all roast beef and Yorkshire pudding for the people of the sceptered isle. English ingenuity has developed some mighty tasty and traditional delicacies over the past ten centuries or so. For example:

English Cheese Pudding

1 quart milk	2 tablespoons butter
2 cups soft bread crumbs	2 cups finely chopped
1 teaspoon salt	cheddar
¼ teaspoon pepper	¼ teaspoon baking soda
2 eggs	

Preheat oven to 350°. Scald the milk. Add bread crumbs, salt, pepper, and butter, and stir until blended. Add the cheese, baking soda, and eggs, well beaten. Transfer to one large or six individual pudding dishes or ramekins rubbed with butter. Place in a pan of hot water and bake at 350° for 45 minutes, or until a knife when inserted comes out clean. Serves 6.

English Scrapple

Good, hot, and cheap — that's a three-word description of scrapple, an old favorite but long forgotten breakfast food. Scrapple is merely a cereal made from some kind — almost any kind — of grain (cornmeal, oats, etc.) cooked and then cooled in a loaf pan, sliced and fried in butter or oil. It costs very little and makes a hearty way to begin the day.

Swedish Food

From Kristin Lavransdatter down, the Swedish people have made much of their sea-girded, chilly domain. Robust rye and tasty fish from icy waters are a mainstay of their healthful diet.

Sweet Swedish Loaf

1 compressed yeast cake
1 cup tepid water
1½ cups scalded milk
3 cups whole wheat flour
1 teaspoon salt
additional flour

¾ cup melted butter
3 eggs
¼ cup honey
1½ tablespoons ground cardamon seeds

Preheat oven to 350° or 375°. Dissolve the yeast in the water; add to the milk. Beat in the flour and salt. Cover and let rise until spongy. In another bowl beat together the butter, eggs, and honey, and add to the dough. Add half the cardamon seeds and the additional flour and knead. Transfer to long, narrow, buttered pans; cover and let rise until doubled in size. Bake at 350° to 375° for about 45 minutes. When almost done brush over with a cornstarch glaze, honey and the remaining cardamon seeds. To make the glaze, add two tablespoons cornstarch to one cup cold water; stir until it looks clear.

A European Chicken-Saver
Fricassee is the traditional European dish designed for extracting the last and the best from an old, tired laying chicken (it works for old, tough turkeys too).

Fricassee

1 stewing chicken (organic)
3 cups water or stock
1 carrot
1 medium onion
1 bay leaf
3 peppercorns
¼ pound mushrooms
12 small onions, peeled

6 tablespoons butter
3 tablespoons flour
2 egg yolks
3 tablespoons cream
fresh parsley, chopped
your choice of herbs
pinch of salt
2 large leeks, sliced

Chapter Fifteen
Recipes From Around The World

Cut up the chicken; place pieces in a large cast iron pot and cover with 3 cups boiling water or veal or chicken stock. Add to the pot the medium onion, carrot, bay leaf, herbs, peppercorns, and leeks. Cover but allow steam to vent. Simmer until tender, usually 1 hour or more. Take out pieces of chicken, keep them hot. Strain stock and chill it. Meanwhile, simmer the 12 small onions and mushrooms in a sauce of 3 tablespoons butter and chicken stock. Now melt 3 tablespoons butter and chicken stock. Cook gently for 10 minutes, remove from fire and correct seasoning. Combine egg yolks with cream. Place chicken on hot platter. Garnish with onions and mushrooms. Stir cream and egg mixture into hot stock. Return to stove until hot but not boiling. Pour sauce over chicken, garnish with parsley, and serve at once. Serves 6-8. *Note:* To stretch this dish, add some barley.

Chapter Sixteen

Healthful Desserts

From Simple Ingredients

What You'll Learn:

How you can enjoy delicious no-sugar desserts at prices so low you can serve them at every meal.

A good dessert must have several things going for it. First, it should look attractive. It's surprising how easy it is to pretty up good food. Always keep a mixture of walnuts, peanuts, cashews, chopped dried fruits, and sunflower seeds in an airtight container. Sprinkle a handful of the mixture over your finished desserts. They'll spark the appearance and taste of any sweet food. Raisins too are great for adding a little touch of sweetness to many desserts. So are fresh grapes and cherries.

Second, the dessert should be appropriate to the meal: a rich substantial dessert should top off a light repast and a light and airy one should end a robust feast.

Finally, desserts should add something wholesome to your diet. Since you are trying to eat better for less money, think of desserts as an important and integral part of your over-all penny-pinching meal plan. Here are some recipes to give your low-cost meals a special final touch.

Banana Spice Bars

These bars are light as cake, but solidly full of the crunch of sunflower seeds, peanuts, and soy grits. One bar provides 5 grams of useable protein, or 11 to 13 percent of the average daily requirements.

1½ cups mashed very ripe bananas	1 teaspoon allspice
2 eggs	2 teaspoons cinnamon
²/₃ cup honey	½ teaspoon nutmeg
¼ cup oil	½ teaspoon salt
½ cup buttermilk or yogurt	¼ teaspoon cardamon
¼ teaspoon almond extract	1 tablespoon baking powder
2 cups whole wheat flour	
¼ cup soy grits	1 teaspoon baking soda
½ cup chopped peanuts	²/₃ cup sunflower seeds

Preheat oven to 350°. Put the bananas, eggs, honey, oil, buttermilk, and almond extract into your blender; buzz until smooth. In a large mixing bowl stir together all the remaining ingredients; make a deep well and pour in the blender mixture. Combine the mixtures completely, but don't overmix. Pour the batter into two well-oiled 9 x 9 pans. Bake at 350° for 30 to 35 minutes, until the cake is well browned on top, dark around the edges, and pulls away from the sides of the pan. Cut into bars (approximately 18) while the cake is still warm; set the pans on racks to cool.

Chapter Sixteen
Healthful Desserts From Simple Ingredients

(Thanks to Ellen Ewald and her *Recipes for a Small Planet* for this and the next four recipes.)

Gingerbread

A dark molasses gingerbread — delicious with yogurt and fruit. One piece provides 4 grams of useable protein, or about 9 to 10 percent of the average daily requirement.

1¾ cups whole wheat flour
½ cup soy flour, scant
½ teaspoon salt
1 teaspoon baking soda
2 teaspoons baking powder
¾ cup hot water

1 tablespoon freshly grated ginger root
2 eggs, beaten
$1/3$ cup oil or melted butter
1 cup unsulfured molasses

Preheat oven to 325°. Stir the dry ingredients together (include the fresh ginger root here, too). Stir the remaining liquid ingredients together. They won't blend very well, but we just want them to be together. Add the liquid to the dry mixture and blend with a few swift strokes. Immediately place the mixture in a well-oiled 9 x 9 baking pan. Bake at 325° for 30 to 35 minutes, until the cake is done. About 12 pieces.

Frozen Cream Cheese and Yogurt Pie

A luscious pie that's easy to assemble. Keep it frozen or it will turn to soup. Garnish with any fresh fruit that's in season. One portion provides about 5 grams of usable protein, 11 to 13 percent of the average daily requirement.

Make one 9" pie crust using 2 cups whole wheat flour, 2 tablespoons milk powder, $2/3$ cup yogurt. Sift dry ingredients, cut in moist ingredients, mix and roll as in regular pastry recipe.

1 cup cream cheese, softened at room temperature — try to obtain cream cheese without additives such as vegetable gum

$2/3$ cup yogurt
¼ cup milk powder ($1/3$ cup instant)
½ cup honey

vanilla or almond flavoring, optional
fruit in season

Bake the pie crust at 375° for about 15 minutes. Cook it while you make the filling.

Beat the cream cheese and yogurt together with a wire whisk (or electric mixer, if you prefer) until the mixture is smooth. Whisk in the milk powder 2 tablespoons at a time; then whisk in the honey. (Add a few drops of flavoring if you wish. You might try lemon or orange, too.) Pour the filling into the cooled pie shell and put it into the freezer. If you are fond of frozen fruit, you may garnish the pie before freezing. Otherwise, when the pie is firm, garnish with fruit and then serve.

Bread Pudding with Lemon Sauce

Make this pudding with whole wheat bread or whole protein bread that has dried out a little. One portion provides about 8 grams of usable protein, or 18 to 22 percent of the average daily requirement.

2 cups dry whole wheat bread cubes
4 cups hot milk
½ to $2/3$ cup honey
1 tablespoon butter

½ teaspoon salt
4 eggs, slightly beaten
1 teaspoon vanilla
½ cup raisins, optional

Preheat oven to 350°. Pour the hot milk over the bread cubes; while they soak, stir in the honey, butter, vanilla, salt and raisins. When the mixture has cooled slightly, beat in the eggs. Pour into an oiled 1½ quart baking dish. Place in a plan of hot water and bake at 350° for about 1 hour, until firm.

While pudding is baking prepare lemon sauce:

1 tablespoon cornstarch	¼ to ⅓ cup honey
dash of salt	1½ tablespoons lemon juice
dash of nutmeg	
1 cup boiling water	2 tablespoons butter

Combine the cornstarch, salt, and nutmeg in a small saucepan; stir in the hot water gradually and cook over low heat until thick and clear. Blend in the honey, lemon juice, and butter. Pour over warm pudding and serve. Makes 8 portions.

Spiced Fruit Rice Pudding

A rice pudding with a difference. One portion provides about 9 grams of usable protein, or 20 to 24 percent of the average daily requirement.

1½ cups raw brown rice	1 egg beaten
2½ to 3 cups milk	½ teaspoon cinnamon
pinch of salt	½ teaspoon nutmeg
½ cup honey	2 tablespoons lemon juice
2 cups of fruit (fresh or soaked dried apples, apricots, or oranges), coarsely chopped	1 cup yogurt
	½ teaspoon powdered ginger

Preheat oven to 350°. Cook the rice in a pressure cooker or regular saucepan, using milk instead of water. Use 2½ cups milk in the pressure cooker or 3 cups in saucepan. When cooked the rice should be tender but will look soupier than rice cooked with water. Stir in the honey, egg, cinnamon, nutmeg and ginger. Oil a 1-quart casserole and spread ½ of the rice mixture over the bottom. Gently place ½ of the fruit chunks on top of the rice. Repeat the two layers and place in a 350° oven. Bake the pudding for 25 minutes. Remove from the oven and spread the 1 cup yogurt over the top. Chill several hours before serving.

Peach Crisp

6 cups fresh or canned peaches, drained
1/3 cup whole wheat flour
1 cup rolled oats

1/4 cup honey
1 teaspoon cinnamon
1/3 cup melted butter

Preheat oven to 375°. Place peaches in baking dish. Combine dry ingredients, add melted butter, mixing until crumbly. Sprinkle on top of peaches. Bake at 375° for 30 minutes or until peaches are tender. Serve warm or cold with cream. To vary, substitute apples for peaches.

Chapter Seventeen

A Checklist Of Health

And Money-Saving Hints

What You'll Learn:
Many practical ways of combatting high food prices and assuring health simultaneously.

As we grew older, it became obvious that health was the real priority in life. Sure, money was needed for daily living but what was really of peak importance was well-being. And if food could assure it, then let's have the best. Live and Learn!

That's why we have completely rewritten this chapter tossing out the meat and margarine and several other no-no's. If we happen to have missed a "bacon drippings" or "shortening," please eliminate it yourself and we thank you.

Name Change Needed

When people died from eating Jack-In-The-Box hamburgers afflicted with E. coli bacteria, I was convinced that the name of the fast-food establishment should be changed to Jack-In-The-Pine-Box.

Meat in America is a scary and sinister substance. Animals are regularly shot with all kinds of weird chemicals. Traces remain when you ingest the meat and a feeling of weirdness can result. Furthermore, the strongest strains of bacteria survive therapeutic doses given to slaughter animals and these are the ones that we humans must now confront. Also, pesticides used in animal food are carried over in the meat that you eat. Did you know that Canada does not allow importation of American meat?

Then there are the spiritual and humanitarian aspects. We should be kind to animals, not eat them.

The Revolution In Nutrition

"Vegetarianism is not a diet. It is a philosophy for healthful eating that eliminates all foods of animal origin plus all refined and processed foods. There remains a wide choice of delicious foods from which to choose at every meal."

— Norman Ford

Vegetarian Diet Anyone?

Some Chileans I've heard of carry 200 pounds of ore up a steep eighty-yard slope twelve times a day. These same people live on a diet of vegetables, figs, bread, and farrenai root (whatever that

Chapter Seventeen
A Checklist Of Health And Money-Saving Hints

is). NO meat. In Brazil, some coffee workers carry a bag of coffee weighing 180 pounds for a mile without resting. Breakfast is figs and bread, lunch boiled beans, dinner roasted wheat. You be the judge. Be advised.

Many nutrition experts tell us that meat has been oversold as a source of protein. It's expensive, acid-forming, and usually loaded with chemicals. According to a recent book, *The Secret Life Of Plants,* meat sometimes has as many as 16 hormones, drugs, and chemicals in it, none of which have a beneficial effect on the consumer. On the contrary, one in particular, DES (diethyl stilbestrol) is carcinogenic. Thus, with so many fine sources of vegetable protein available, it becomes highly conjectural whether meat should be eaten at all.

On a more positive plane, consider the facts presented in that same book regarding the radiations from various foods. As a basis of comparison, the radiations from humans are rated at 6,500 angstroms (an angstrom is a measure of wavelength). Foods are divided into four general classes, high radiation being preferable to low. Fruits and vegetables at the peak of maturity and freshness rate from 8,000 to 10,000 angstroms. They achieve the highest rating when consumed raw. Wheat has a radiance of 8,500 angstroms and rises to 9,000 when cooked. Olive oil, butter (when fresh), and fresh seafood and fish also rate high: 8,000 angstroms and up.

In the second class of foods are such items as eggs, peanut oil, boiled vegetables and cooked fish. These rate from 6,500 down to 3,000 angstroms. Of meats, the only one to make the 6,500 and up category is freshly smoked ham. The others are "pointless to eat, an exercise in tough digestion which wears out rather than revitalizes the eater," according to the above-mentioned book.

The third category includes all cooked meats, coffee, tea, jams, fermented cheeses and white bread. Because of their low radiation they do one little or no good. At the bottom, dead as far as radiation is concerned, are margarines, preserves, alcohol, refined sugar and bleached white flour.

Eat Well For 99¢ A Meal

There are many fine books on vegetarianism versus omnivorism. These include:

Let's Eat Right To Keep Fit, Adelle Davis, Harcourt Brace Jovanovich.
Food Is Your Best Medicine, H.G. Bieler, MD, Random House.
Diet For A Small Planet, F.M. Lappé, Ballantine Books.
The Natural Food Cookbook, B. Hunter, Simon and Schuster.
The Complete Book Of Foods And Nutrition, J.I. Rodale, Rodale Press.
The Secret Life Of Plants, Peter Tompkins & Christopher Bird, Harper & Row.

Study of these volumes will probably convince you that a strictly vegetable diet can be healthy. It is even more convincing to try a vegetarian way of life for several months. Then make your own decision. That's what I did and now enjoy a virtually meatless (and thus less expensive) way of life! Health and energy levels have never been higher!

Beware The Forever Fruit

Did you hear about the maraschino cherry that was buried in the ground for years and dug up good as new? That's just about what would happen to most supermarket foods if they were buried. So imagine how they must lie in your stomach daring a digestive juice to penetrate their preservatives!

Versatile Vegetables

Most of the vitamins and nutrients in vegetables are in or near the skin. And nearly all vegetables are edible from root to stem. So wash all vegetables before peeling, (if you must peel) place the

Chapter Seventeen
A Checklist Of Health And Money-Saving Hints

parings in the freezer and wrap in cheesecloth to add to simmering soups. For stocks, no other vegetables are needed.

Don't throw away the dandelions from your lawn; you can eat both leaves and root, cooked or in salad.

Fennel grows in abundance all over the world. Collect it yourself and cook the stems like celery, add mushrooms, tomatoes and olive oil, Italian style.

Eggplant is usually a good buy and it's nutritious too. Tasty when stewed with onions, tomatoes, and green peppers. Even better when prepared like a small steak; dipped in a fritter batter and sautéed. Adding Parmesan cheese makes them superb and even children, the fussy type, will eat them.

Your Daily Dollar

With dairy foods skyrocketing in price over the past ten years, it's time to learn how to obtain the most from the least.

Powdered milk is your best buy. A dash of vanilla may be added to improve the taste, or mix powdered milk with whole raw milk to stretch the quantity. Powdered milk tastes best when prepared a day in advance and refrigerated overnight before drinking.

Eggs, bought when they are less expensive, may be successfully frozen for use in baking or scrambling. Wrap the yolks and whites separately to freeze.

Whipping cream is expensive. Add a ripe, mashed banana to an egg white and beat until stiff for an economical substitute.

A low cost substitute for sour cream is yogurt. See the recipe given earlier in this book. Use yogurt on baked potatoes or any place where sour cream is often used.

Eggs have the highest protein content per pound. Be sure they come from free-running, organically grown, happy chickens. Once you enjoy a real egg, you'll know the difference.

To the Last Crumb

Grind toast into dry bread crumbs in your blender; soft bread crumbs can be made from leftover bread or crusts. Store in airtight containers.

Make seasoned crumbs for many uses by adding dry minced onion, seasoned salt, pepper and/or herbs.

Do It Yourself and Save

Make-ahead mixes and prepared foods are convenient but they cost more. In many cases, you can make up your own combinations in bulk. And stored properly, they will keep indefinitely.

Seasoned salt is a combination of ¼ cup salt, 2 tablespoons paprika, 1½ teaspoons pepper, 1½ teaspoons onion powder.

Onion salt may be made by grinding dried, minced onion flakes to a powder in the electric blender and mixing to taste with table salt.

Save about 30 cents per pound by making your own noodles. Use a fork or slotted spoon to mix a cup of whole wheat flour with two eggs and 1 teaspoon salt. Roll thin, cut into strips and dry.

Save money by making your own tomato juice. To one small can of tomato paste (6 ounces), add celery seed, salt and enough water to make one quart; mix well.

Make your own cream soups by puréeing leftover vegetables and broth with evaporated milk in the electric blender. Worcestershire sauce or curry powder may be added to your taste.

Creamed salad dressings may be made by adding herbs, spices, and/or cheese to yogurt.

Add vinegar and oil to nearly empty catsup or chili sauce bottles for French-type salad dressing.

Miscellaneous

Soak whole grain overnight. In the morning, grind it or place in a blender. Add raisins, nuts, dates or other good things. Eat hot or cold with or without milk and honey. Inexpensive and nutritious.

Chapter Seventeen
A Checklist Of Health And Money-Saving Hints

Is there a spaghetti factory near you? If so, buy their broken pieces for a fraction of the price of regular spaghetti. Sometimes they sell their "bends," the looped part, for very little, and they taste just as good as the "straights" when cooked.

To make your own biscuit mix, combine 8 cups whole wheat flour, $1^1/_3$ cups non-fat dry milk, 5 tablespoons salt (optional). Work in 1 cup shortening with fingertips until mixture resembles fine meal. Store in airtight container in cool, dry place.

Earn some extra money by canning wild blackberries with homemade labels. You'll sell all you make.

When strawberries are in season, find a roadside stand selling them by the flat.

Eat Well For 99¢ A Meal

Swiss chard is the most prolific plant you can grow in your backyard garden. Plant some soon and reap a continual harvest. Good cooked with salt, pepper and butter or cooked/chilled with any salad dressing.

Ever try set line fishing? Just bait some hooks on a single line, drop in the water from a bleach bottle float and go about your business. The fish will catch themselves and wait for your return.

Saving Substitutions

Canned mackerel may be substituted for salmon, especially in casserole recipes.

Oatmeal makes a fine substitute for expensive nuts. A good example of the usage is in pecan pie.

Save money on baby food by puréeing vegetables and fruits from your regular dinner with a little liquid for baby.

Save the pickle liquid for use in potato salad. Or when the pickles are gone, add fresh vegetables such as carrot sticks, onions, green peppers or cucumbers to the jar and pickle your own treat.

If Your Cupboard Looks Like Mother Hubbard's...

Down to your last dollar? We were one summer, so we bought nothing but potatoes and onions. We boiled up a batch of the spuds and used them with whatever else we could scrounge up. Often we caught fish from San Francisco Bay (we were living on a boat). When we acquired a little more money from odd jobs, we bought a twenty-five pound sack of brown rice. We boiled rice for breakfast and added chopped fruit salvaged from the produce market. For lunch we had cold rice with bits of home-smoked fish and some soy sauce. Another big batch of rice was boiled up for dinner, and

Chapter Seventeen
A Checklist Of Health And Money-Saving Hints

a mound of it was heaped high with more scavenging — this time celery and chard to make a passable imitation of a Chinese vegetable dish. Soy sauce helped out immeasurably; it lends a meaty taste to everything. Do you get the picture? Have some solid basic foods around with which to build the menu, meal, or snack. It's analogous to building a log cabin with the trees you find in a nearby forest. With the basic materials handy, it's not hard to provide the trimmings.

The Optimum

Imagine the fertile garden, far from the city, where you grow just about everything you need. Want a salad? Harvest the leaves of a young romaine or butter lettuce, some crisp carrots and a still-warm-from-the-sun tomato. Toss with a homemade dressing of olive oil, Balsamic vinegar and fresh chopped basil.

Once you enjoy a salad like this, you'll want one every day.

Speaking of olive oil, it's become our favorite for every purpose from salads to popcorn, from a dip for French bread to the crowning touch of Coq au Vin.

Not as expensive as one would think, especially if purchased in those 3 liter tins. There are also grades from Pomace to Extra Virgin... the latter being best for salad dressing and the popcorn adornment.

Furthermore, it keeps well and is lots healthier than most oils on the market.

Outdoor Cooking

Nothing tastes better than a meal cooked over a campfire. Stews, soups and casseroles are easy and lend themselves to long-term simmering over a fire down to coals. Don't forget to put some potatoes in the hot ashes for a wonderful treat. Brush them off, split open, slather with butter or olive oil and herbs and become a wilderness gourmet.

Upping Protein

You can raise the protein level of many foods by combining them in various ways. Great ways to enjoy more protein without eating hazardous meat. For example, rice or beans eaten separately produce a modest level of protein. But if you eat them together, there is a 43 percent increase in usable protein! This is explained in detail in the classic book by Francis Lappé titled *Diet For A Small Planet*, a Ballantine original. You'll find it in most libraries.

A companion volume with many more recipes is *Recipes For A Small Planet* by Ellen Ewald.

The Killers

Hydrogenated fats consist of oils into which hydrogen atoms have been forced to make them solid. Any degree of hydrogenation causes a change in molecular structure which increases the risk of heart disease, stroke, hypertension and other lethal ailments.

So read the labels and if there is any hydrogenated oil, partial or otherwise, put the item back on the shelf and mosey on. Worst offenders are margarine, salad dressings, peanut butter and most commercial baked goods.

Chapter Seventeen
A Checklist Of Health And Money-Saving Hints

We all need protein but unfortunately the average American diet provides three times as much as we need. Cancers of the lymph system, brain and nervous systems have been associated with excessive intake of animal protein.

The average man requires only three ounces of plant protein per day. This can be readily supplied by a well-complemented mix of seeds, legumes, nuts, whole grains, fruits, veggies and sprouts.

Whether you like it or not, processed food contains many kinds of additives placed there for the benefit of manufacturers. Any packaged or canned food contains preservatives, color, bleaches, stabilizers, taste enhancers and so forth, most of which have never been tested.

Nathan Pritikin said it best ... he called processed food "cosmetized garbage." It looks good and even tastes good but basically it can be defined as garbage, being worthless nutritionally and harmful to varying degrees.

As this is written, the average dose of additives is about 10 pounds per year per person. It's so easy to pass up this killer dose... just pass up all processed foods!

Lesser Known Seasonings

The desire for a meat-like taste is often hard to overcome since so many of us have been programmed to accept meat in its many forms. However, there are flavorful additions which provide lots of flavor at low cost and with no harmful side effects.

MISO: Derived from soy, this paste-like seasoning is offered in various compositions and can be purchased in bulk. So try several until you find a favorite. Useful in making soups, sauces and stews but can be added to almost anything that would benefit from a little more flavor and taste.

GOMASIO: To make this Japanese seasoning, toast sesame seeds and grind with sea salt at about a 15 to 1 ratio.

Eat Well For 99¢ A Meal

TAHINI: Also made from Sesame, this is a very appealing seasoning that you can buy from most oriental, gourmet or New Age food stores.

SESAME OIL: Sold in small bottles, this is one of our favorite additions to stir-frys or any Oriental dishes. Though expensive, it's the ultimate oil and you need little to add a lot of taste.

TEMPEH: A soy and grain combination that has a wonderful robust flavor which is the result of yeast action. Can be enjoyed in many delightful forms including as a "burger" patty.

FALAFEL MIX: We buy this not so much for falafels but to use as a seasoning. Just a sprinkle or two will transform most blah dishes.

CURRY POWDER: There are infinite varieties of this Indian seasoning which often contain ten or more spices and herbs. May be added to almost any dish for increased flavor and interest.

CAYENNE: Love this hot spice derived from those red-hot peppers. We keep a shaker close by and generate lots of taste with just a few grains.

PUMPKIN SEEDS: MEN! Want to avoid prostate trouble? Just eat a few tablespoons of fresh pumpkin seeds daily. Lots of natural vitamin E and essential oils make this a no-prescription cure and no side effects either!

NUTRITIONAL OR BREWER'S YEAST: Our frenetic world requires nerves of steel. One way to have them is to supply your system with plenty of the B vitamins and trace minerals. Easy to take; just add a tablespoon or two to raw milk or fruit juice.

SAUERKRAUT: Countries with lots of centenarians also have lots of fermented foods available. One of the best and cheapest is sauerkraut which you can make yourself.

Chapter Seventeen
A Checklist Of Health And Money-Saving Hints

A ceramic or glass container of the desired size is the main piece of equipment. Shred cabbage thinly and layer it with a bit of salt, some cayenne and cumin. You can also add strips of raw vegetables because they'll be pickled by the juice.

1. Compress sliced cabbage.
2. When container is full, cover with cloth and weight with a stone.
3. Let ferment for a week or two, removing foam and replacing cloth.
4. When fermentation stops, store in refrigerator in glass jars.

Enjoy it raw although it can be cooked in many ways. Keeps almost forever and is a great wintertime veggie.

RUSSIAN RYE: With that homemade kraut, enjoy some real rye bread made as follows. This bread may account for the longevity of Russian peasants.

Mix 8 cups of freshly ground rye flour with 3 cups of warm water and a half cup of sourdough starter. The latter is available at almost any health food store. Let rise overnight in a warm place such as an oven with pilot light. Add more flour if needed and knead well. Place in baking pans and allow to double in bulk. Bake about one hour at 350° F. Remove and cool on wire rack.

Not only is this bread super tasty, it will provide a workout for your teeth. Spread with sweet butter or some caraway-seeded Monterey Jack cheese.

VITAMIN C: Linus Pauling almost made it to a hundred himself by taking substantial quantities of C. Here's what it can do for you:
- Stimulates your glandular system and helps produce hormones.
- Protects you from being poisoned, internally and externally.
- Keeps collagen healthy thus maintaining youthful skin.
- Can prevent arteriosclerosis.

- Vital to the functioning of sex glands, both in men and women.

So stir up some powdered C in fruit juice and assure health.

OPEN SESAME: We use them on buns but in the Middle East sesame seeds are a staple food which:
- Has more calcium than milk.
- More protein than meat.
- Has the good-guy unsaturated fatty acids and Vitamins B, E.
- Has lots of lecithin.
- Can be used as a garnish, as a flavorful oil, in tahini sauce and as a wonderful candy, halvah. Make your own by grinding a cup of seeds and mixing it with two teaspoons of honey until it forms a stiff dough. Smooth out in a small pan about ¼ inch thick and cut into bars.

KEFIR: This cultured milk has been around for many centuries helping people cope with age. Similar to yogurt but thinner in consistency, you can make it in your own kitchen using "kefir grains" bought from your local health or natural food store.

MUESLI: Imitations of this Swiss cereal appear on grocery shelves but you can make it fresh and as good as the Bircher-Benner Clinic does. For a single portion, soak two tablespoons of regular rolled oats in twice the quantity of water overnight. In the morning, shred two apples and add to oats along with two tablespoons of chopped almonds and skim milk and honey to taste. Stir vigorously and eat promptly. A breakfast like this will have you full of energy. If you wish, add a sprinkle of wheat germ and bran.

RAW FOODS: One of the most successful doctors to practice in America was the late Alan Hopkins Nittler, MD. He healed thousands of people of myriad diseases most often using nothing but diet as the cure. One of his strong recommendations was to eat about 80 percent of your food in its raw state... raw veggies, fruits, seeds, nuts, and so forth.

Chapter Seventeen
A Checklist Of Health And Money-Saving Hints

Not only do you save your health, you save a lot of time and fuel. Think about it, what animals cook their food?

VITAMINS AND MINERALS: If taking these essential elements of diet in pill form bothers you, then try this. Grind and mix dates, figs, sunflower seeds, various nuts and similar items into bars. Eat small amounts daily and enjoy what your body needs in a delicious form. Again, no cooking required.

THE RINSE FORMULA: Most Americans have a degree of arteriosclerosis or hardening of the arteries. A healthy way to combat his situation is to eat a portion of this formula daily. It was developed by Dr. Jacobus Rinse.

For two cups of mix, combine $1/2$ cup each of bran, rolled oats and wheat germ with $3/8$ cup of lecithin and $1/8$ cup of sunflower seeds plus one tablespoon each of brewer's yeast and bone meal. Keep in the refrigerator because the wheat germ becomes rancid otherwise.

Serve with fruits, nuts and skim milk that has been blended with a teaspoon of an unsaturated oil such as cold-processed safflower oil.

KELP: Don't worry about getting necessary minerals. You can buy powdered kelp at any natural food store. Keep it in a shaker on your table and use like salt and pepper. A sea veggie, it contains almost every known mineral.

ANOTHER SHAKER IDEA: I learned that cayenne pepper keeps old people frisky. So a shaker is next to my place mat. In this way you can control the heat of any dish to any desired degree.

THE FOREVER FOOD: Do you know that parrots live to be 100 years old or more on a diet of just sunflower seeds and water?

OUTWITTING OBSOLESCENCE

Change is accelerating, so reading current publications is necessary to keep up. Try some of these food, health and data sources.

Chili Pepper, the Magazine of Spicy Foods, Out West Publishing, PO Box 80780, Albuquerque, NM 87198-0780. Hot chili peppers are used world-wide to spark up the taste appeal of veggies. We buy our peppers in their natural dried form and either grind or toss in whole.

Eating Well, PO Box 1001, Charlotte, VT 05445-1001. A fine newer magazine featuring both domestic and foreign cuisine concepts. In a recent issue, they reviewed fennel and gave a recipe for Parmesan Crostini... mmm!

Vegetarian Gourmet, Chitra Publications, 2 Public Avenue, Montrose, PA 18801. The name tells it all.

Let's Live, Hilltopper Publications, 320 N Larchmont, PO Box 74908, Los Angeles, CA 90004-3030. Long-lived magazine with a diversity of relevant data on health.

Vegetarian Times, 4 High Ridge Park, Stamford, CT 06905. Makes a good case for building healthy body with veggies.

Health Freedom News, PO Box 688, Monrovia, CA 91017. Publication of the esteemed National Health Federation with convincing evidence that the government is playing games with us regarding food. And if we have the wrong data, we lose.

Speaking of data, here are some magazines for those with personal computers and modems, the fastest way to acquire all kinds of vital information.

Online Access, Magazine that Makes the Modems Work, 920 Franklin, Ste. 203, Chicago, IL 60610. Just what it says.

Chapter Seventeen
A Checklist Of Health And Money-Saving Hints

Byte, 1 Phoenix Mill Lane, Peterborough, NH 03458-0809. The recurring bible of the PC world. Ads alone will keep you up to date.

Wired, 544 Second Street, San Francisco, CA 94107. The avant garde computer magazine not averse to whistle blowing. Deserves our support.

Recommended Reading

It is strongly suggested that the reader who wishes to not only save money but enjoy better health take the time to study as many of these books as possible. Check the library or order through your local bookstores, new or used.

The Complete Book of Food and Nutrition. J.I. Rodale and staff. Rodale Books. Emmaus, PA, 1961. A monumental work by a most astute researcher who was probably zapped by the food industry for his efforts to alert the American people. Read it if you don't read another book in this bibliography.

Let's Have Children; Let's Get Well; Let's Eat Right; Let's Cook It Right. Signet, New American Library. Bergenfield, NJ. These four books by the late Adelle Davis warrant a place front and center in your personal library.

Back To Eden. Jethro Kloss. The date of the original copyright is 1939, but material from this book has been extensively reprinted. Longview Publishing House, Coalmont, TN. Subtitled, *A Human Interest Story of Health and Restoration to Be Found in Herb, Root and Bark,* this quaint volume presents such homely advice as "Eat food as far as possible in its natural state." Advises against the use of aluminum pots and for the consumption of nuts instead of meats.

The Natural Foods Cookbook. B.T. Hunter. Pyramid Books, NY, 1961. Hard to believe that this has been around so long, but then, it takes a while to sell a million copies. That should be recommendation enough.

Stalking the Wild Asparagus. Euell Gibbons. David McKay, NY, 1962. This and Gibbons' other volumes — *Stalking the Healthful Herb, Stalking the Blue-Eyed Scallop,* and *Beachcombers Handbook* — were the top sellers about gathering wild things to eat. And as prices continue to rise on through the ceiling, Gibbons' books become ever more relevant; we can even forgive him for having done TV commercials.

An Herb and Spice Cookbook. C. Clairborne. Harper and Row, NY, 1964. A must for the person who wants lots of flavor in his non-meat diet.

The Gourmet Health Foods Cookbook. M. and O. Teichner. Coronet, NY, 1967. Divided into two sections, "Magic Without Meat," and "Savor Without Salt," this modest volume will add to your resources as a vegetarian and salt-free cook.

International Vegetarian Cookery. S. Richmond. Arco Publishing, NY, 1970. Covers the world effectively and cites some unusual ways of making vegetables taste like they should.

Foods, Facts and Fallacies. C. Fredericks, PhD. Arco Publishing, NY, 1969. The author has been a pioneer in the field of eating healthy foods; this book reflects recent research in nutrition and health.

Recommended Reading

The Soybean Cookbook. D. Jones. Arco Publishing, NY, 1971. Since soybeans are a worthy replacement for meat, the 350 recipes herein will extend your interest substantially in the good bean.

Get Well Naturally. Linda Clark. Arco Publishing, NY, 1972. Ms. Clark also wrote *Stay Young Forever* and cites the nutritional ways to better health and longer life in both volumes.

Deaf Smith County Cookbook. M.W. Ford. Collier Books, NY, 1973. This cookbook invites substitution of good food in your present recipes.

The Vegetarian Epicure. A. Thomas, Vintage Books, NY, 1972. More than 2540 recipes that make vegetables taste good.

Vegetarian Gourmet Cookery. A. Hooker. Scribner & Sons, NY, 1973. Another good book on living without meat.

Diet For A Small Planet. F.M. Lappé. Ballantine Books, NY, 1971. This is the original book that revealed how you can put together vegetable proteins to make protein-rich meals without meats. An overall plan for eating less or no meat. A breakthrough that makes other cookbooks obsolete.

Recipes For A Small Planet. E. B. Ewald. Ballantine Books, NY, 1973. The companion volume to the blockbusting *Diet For A Small Planet.* Read it by all means!

Middle Eastern Cookery. E. Zane. Scribner & Sons, NY, 1974. Turkish, Armenian, North African, and Persian recipes utilizing the traditional ingredients — kasha, chicken, fish, fruits, vegetables, and rice.

The Sweet Life. M. Newman. Houghton Mifflin, NY, 1974. Without using a bit of sugar or refined flour or any milk, the author has created great desserts from fruit juices, whole grain flours, natural sweeteners and unrefined vegetable oils.

Mental Health Through Nutrition. T. R. Blaine. Citadel Division of Lyle Stuart, NY, 1974. The layman's guide to attaining and keeping mental health through nutrition. It's a study of how vitamin and mineral deficiencies are responsible for most of our physical and mental ills.

Cookbook For Good Nutrition. Carlton Fredericks. Grosset & Dunlap, NY, 1974. An old-timer in the struggle for better quality foods, Fredericks continues his mission to keep Americans from committing gastronomic suicide. A diversified book emphasizing that good nutrition can be fun.

A Basket Of Homemade Breads. U. Norman. Morrow, NY, 1973. A highly pictorial how-to-do-it bread book.

The *Vegetarian Menu Cookbook.* E. Michaels. Drake Publishers, NY, 1973. Heavily illustrated, this book shows the great beauty of non-meat cooking.

Madame Wu's Art of Chinese Cooking. Charles Publishing Co., Los Angeles, CA, 1973. Aristocratic, well illustrated, and a handsome addition to a Chinese cookery library.

Chinese Cooking For Beginners. A. Schryver. Dodd Mead, NY, 1974. Combines interesting fresh vegetables and very small amounts of poultry and meat or fish; an excellent introduction to the world's oldest cuisine.

Encyclopedia of Chinese Food and Cooking. W. and I. Chang. Crown Publishers, NY, 1970. Useful for its inventory of Chinese ingredients, photographs and descriptions.

Recommended Reading

Making Your Own Cheese and Yogurt. M. Alth. Funk & Wagnalls, NY, 1973. And why not, if you have lots of milk around?

The Rodale Cookbook. N. Albright. Rodale Press, Emmaus, PA, 1973. Photographically enhanced, this large volume reflects the careful thinking of the pioneer Rodale group.

The Organic Directory. Rodale Press, Emmaus, PA, 1974. A listing of places to buy organic and natural food supplies. Both producers and purveyors are presented.

The New York Times Natural Foods Cookbook. J. Hewitt. Quadrangle Books, NY, 1971. Over 700 recipes without artificial flavors, colors, or chemicals.

The Secret of the Seeds, Vegetables, Fruits and Nuts. B. Friedlander. Grosset & Dunlap, NY, 1974. How you can recognize, grow, buy, prepare, eat, and enjoy vegetables, fruits and nuts.

The New York Times Bread and Soup Cookbook. Y.Y. Tarr. Quadrangle Books, NY, 1972. This book emphasizes a more natural way of living and a more basic way of cooking. Typical are Danish Cabbage Soup and English Cobblestone Bread.

Index

—A—

alcoholic beverages, 86
Angier, Bradford, 77
animal: animal feed, 29

—B—

baked goods, *See* also bread; cakes and cookies; grains
barley, 16, 29, 86
barter, 33
basil, 71; herb, 71
beans, 7, 18, 101
beverage, 83; coffee. *also see*; cola, 83; fruit drinks, 54, 102; grape wine, 87; honey soy drink, 139; tomato juice, 174
beverage recipes, blackberry wine, 44
Bieler: H.G., 172
blender, 174
bread, 124; Boston Brown Bread, 126; buying, 26; crumbs, 174; quick and easy, 101; Russian Rye, 181; salt rising, 125; sourdough, 103, 124, 181; uses for, 102; wheat berry, 126; whole grain, 98; yeast, 102

—C—

caffeine, 83, 85
calcium, 4, 23, 69, 93, 94, 182
candy, vi, 17, 94, 182
candy, cakes, and cookies, 84
carbohydrates, 3, 100
cheese, 3, 12, 19, 26, 27, 34, 52, 70, 99, 105, 131
Chinese food, 10, 18, 53, 54, 148, 177, 190
chives, 69, 70
coffee, 12, 24, 85, 112, 116, 171; grinders, 56
cola, 83, 93, 94
Collins: Dr. D.A., 83
condiment receipes: Homemade Salsa, 120; Potato Mayonnaise, 110; Wild Apple Vinegar, 109
corn, 17, 29, 69, 124
Cornaro: Luigi, 97

—D—

Dahl: Frances, 92
dairy, 37, 156, 173
Danish food, 157
Davis, Adelle, 6, 84, 172, 187;
dessert recipes, 120; Banana Spice Bars, 164; Blackberry Pie, 45; Blackberry Slump, 44; Bread

Pudding with Lemon Sauce, 166; Danish Apfelskiver, 157; Frozen Cream Cheese and Yogurt Pie, 165; Gingerbread, 165; Honey-Almond Brown Rice Delight, 106; Peach Crisp, 120; Plain scones, 158; Rose Hip Jam, 42; Scotch Shortbread, 158; Scotch Toast with Honey, 114; Spiced Fruit Rice Pudding, 167; Steamed French Bread pudding, 152
dill, 70, 78

—E—

egg recipes: Huevos Rancheros, 145; Shrimp egg foo yung, 149
eggs, 23, 171, 173; preserving, 79
English food, 159
ethnic cooking, 143
Ewald, Ellen, 165

—F—

fats: and diet needs, 22, 100; and starches, 85; in soybeans, 18
feed stores, 26, 29
fireless cooker, 51, 52
fish, 23, 101; buying of, 34, 38; raw, 150; smoked, 73, 75
fishing, 47, 118, 176
food: attitude towards, 97; bulk buying, 26; buying, iii, 10, 100; Cooperative buying, 26; cost analysis, 104, 108, 110, 113, 115, 117, 119, 121; industry, 4, 187; packaging, 82; packaging of, 37, 57; radiations from, 171; storage of, 10, 27, 77, 130; wholesale buying, 26
food growing, 7. *See* Gardening
food preservation, 77; canning, 60, 74, 77; drying, 27, 74; freezing, 74, 77; liquid storage, 77, 78; smoking, 75, 77
food staples. *See* staples
free food, 40. *See* wild food
French food, 151
fruit drinks, 102
Fruit of the Month Club, 37
fruits, 23; buying, 32, 33; dried, 163

—G—

gardening: books, 67; harvesting, 66; mulching, 65; seeds, 68, 69, 70; space, 64; sprouts, 23, 68, 179; transplanting, 62; window boxes, 64
garlic, 22
German food, 150
Gibbons: Euell, 188
grain recipes: animal feed cereal, 29; biscuit mix, 175; bread, 125, 126; breads, 107; enchiladas baja, 106; Italian Gnocchi, 147; noodles, 174; pilaf, 154; spaghetti, 147; sweet Swedish loaf, 160; swiss cheese biscuits, 156; western pancakes, 109; whole grain bread, 124
grains: as a staple, 9; as coffee, 85; buying, 7; grinders for, 56

—H—

Health food stores. *See* Natural food stores
herbs, 69, 70, 71, 78, 79, 115
Honey, 23, 31, 91
Hunter: B., 172

—I—

Indian food, 155
iron, 3, 130
Italian food, 146

Index

—J—

Japanese food, 150

—L—

Lappé, F.M., 172, 178, 189;
lecithin, 137, 182
leftovers, 101

—M—

Mayer: Dr. Jean, 93
Menus, 105; balanced, 103; breakfast, 109; round-the-world, 119; seafood, 116; vegetarian, 111
Mexican food, 10, 145
Middle Eastern food, 153
milk, 22; powdered, 173
Millet, 17
mint, 70, 71, 86
molasses, 91, 93
money-saving hints, 5, 27, 33; barter, 10, 33; bulk buying, 26, 27; ethnic stores, 144; for grains, 7, 9; for produce, 32, 33, 36; of meats, 13, 171; spices, 115

—N—

natural flours, 124
natural food stores, 28, 115
natural leavening, 124
Nutrients, 172; table of functions, 2, 3; yield charts for, 23

—O—

oats, 16, 29
onions, 19
overeating, 97, 98

—P—

packaging, 82
peanut butter, 29, 84, 178
potato recipes, 118, 129, 130, 131, 132, 151
potatoes, 101; as a staple, 19, 26; buying, 130; storing, 36
poultry, 23, 114; buying, 114
produce, 32, 36
protein, 178; in soybeans, 137; values of, 18, 23; in vegetarian diet, 171

—R—

radiations, 171
restaurants, 88
rice: brown, 16; white, 16
Rodale, J.I., 67, 84, 93, 172
rye, 17

—S—

sage, 71
salad dressing, 52, 174
salsa, 120
sauces: Béarnaise, 152; Indian, 155
sauerkraut, 180
Scottish food, 158
seasonings, 179
shallots, 22
shopping: cooperatives, 27; for eggs, 173; for produce, 32; for spices, 115; from farms, 32; in bulk, 26; wholesale, 26
snacks, 85, 99
soft drinks, 82, 94
soul food, 154
soup recipes: Barley-Mushroom Soup, 114; chowders, 146; Constantinople Meatless Pepper Pot, 153; curry soup, 156; minestrone, 112;
sourdough starter, 181

soy protein, 137
soybean: as a staple, 18; cost of, 138; nutritive values of, 138
soybean recipes: Soy Burgers, 138; Soybean Shanghai, 150; soybean soufflé, 139
spaghetti, 147, 175
split peas, 18
sprouts, 23, 62
staples, 152; basic, 26; buying, 27
sugar, 6; alternatives of, 23, 84; effects of, 82, 83
Swedish food, 159
Swiss food, 156

—T—

teas: alfalfa, 110; anise, 111; birch, 44; wild mint, 86

—U—

U.S. Army *Survival Guide*, 47
utensils, 49, 50; blender, 52; Chinese, 53; fireless cooker, 51; grinders, 56; tenderizers, 55

—V—

vegetable: proteins in, 171
vegetable recipes: cabbage (red), 150; cactus, 41; eggplant, 112; flying goose chow mein, 149; Italian eggplant, 148; potato dumplings, 132; red onion potota salad, 131; refried beans, 112, 145; sauerkraut, 180; potato, 133; soul succotash, 154; sprout, cabbage and green pepper salad, 107; spud and carrot bash, 132; potato, 132; zucchini frittata, 114
vegetables, 10, 22; buying of, 10, 26, 32; damaged, 36, 37; overripe, 32; storage of, 77, 78
vegetarian menus, 111
vitamins, 3, 16, 22, 23, 29, 69, 93, 114

—W—

Walsh: M.H., 93
whole grain wheat, 11, 30
wholesale shopping, 26
wild food, 40, 47, 118; acorn, 40, 46; alfalfa, 68, 86; anise, 111; apple vinegar, 109; birch syrup, 120; blackberries, 39, 44, 175; cactus, 41, 71; cattails, 40; olives, 46; piñon nuts, 43; poke salad, 120; roses, 42; tossed salad, 109
wine, 86; blackberry, 87; grape, 87

—Y—

yogurt, 23, 103, 111, 173; maker, 52
Yudkin: Dr. John, 92